M000218399

Extending Unity with Editor Scripting

Put Unity to use for your video games by creating your own custom tools with editor scripting

Angelo Tadres

BIRMINGHAM - MUMBAI

Extending Unity with Editor Scripting

Copyright © 2015 Packt Publishing

All rights reserved. No part of this book may be reproduced, stored in a retrieval system, or transmitted in any form or by any means, without the prior written permission of the publisher, except in the case of brief quotations embedded in critical articles or reviews.

Every effort has been made in the preparation of this book to ensure the accuracy of the information presented. However, the information contained in this book is sold without warranty, either express or implied. Neither the author, nor Packt Publishing, and its dealers and distributors will be held liable for any damages caused or alleged to be caused directly or indirectly by this book.

Packt Publishing has endeavored to provide trademark information about all of the companies and products mentioned in this book by the appropriate use of capitals. However, Packt Publishing cannot guarantee the accuracy of this information.

First published: September 2015

Production reference: 1150915

Published by Packt Publishing Ltd.
Livery Place
35 Livery Street
Birmingham B3 2PB, UK.

ISBN 978-1-78528-185-3

www.packtpub.com

Credits

Author
Angelo Tadres

Reviewers
J. Alberto Gandullo Avila
Jeremy Jones
Noah Johnson
Fernando Matarrubia
Hugo Ruivo
Eric Spevacek

Commissioning Editor
Veena Pagare

Acquisition Editor
Sonali Vernekar

Content Development Editor
Riddhi Tuljapurkar

Technical Editor
Vivek Pala

Copy Editor
Pranjali Chury

Project Coordinator
Kinjal Bari

Proofreader
Safis Editing

Indexer
Mariammal Chettiyar

Graphics
Jason Monteiro

Production Coordinator
Conidon Miranda

Cover Work
Conidon Miranda

Foreword

While perhaps not as glamorous a job as being a gameplay programmer, a tools programmer can make your game development experience much more enjoyable. They truly are the unsung heroes of game development. In fact, AAA studios heavily rely on using tools to make aspects of game development easier to use for designers and artists. Tools also help to reduce tediousness in the creation of content for game projects.

While these tools were often created as separate programs to be run in conjunction with the game engine in the past, one of the things I love about working with the Unity game engine is the fact that with some fairly trivial scripting, you can extend the editor. This allows users to tailor the editor to suit their project's needs and requirements. Additionally, just as Unity was originally created for a game project but grew into a lot more, the custom tools readers will go on to create applications that have the possibility to be extraordinarily successful on Unity's Asset Store, much like NGUI, Playmaker, ProBuilder, and UFPS.

Since I started working with Unity in 2007, I have worked with a lot of tools and have done a fair bit of tools programming personally. While creating my own tools, I often needed to do extensive external research and come up with a lot of things on my own because most of the necessary information was not documented well. I am exuberant that someone has compiled the majority of this information into one place.

Over the course of this book, you will see how you can create your own custom tools starting with simple ones such as gizmos, then moving on to customize the Inspector for the different components you add, and learning how to create your very own Windows with their own custom GUI. Angelo has broken down the concepts and has made it quite easy to see when you would want to use these tools. Throughout this book, he shows practical examples of when you would want to use these particular features from their inception to getting published on the Asset Store. He has also included additional tips and tricks along the way, such as how to set up Git, easily make multiple builds of your projects, as well as get your project up on mobile devices in a flash.

Reading Angelo's work, I am not surprised by the range of content covered in this book. His work as a lead engineer for DeNA as well as his strong technical background, no doubt, gave him the knowledge needed to get this book out to the world. The breadth of content included in this book will give you a strong foundation on which you can build your own tools.

Gifted tools programmers can make all the difference in the world of game projects. This book provides a roadmap on how you can get there.

John P. Doran

Technical Game Designer

Author of Unity Game Development Blueprints and Mastering UDK Game Development

About the Author

Angelo Tadres is a Chilean software engineer, living the dream of working in the mobile video game industry.

Hailing from Santiago, Chile, he began his career doing research and development for video games and applications that are designed to assist the blind and visually impaired with their orientation and mobility skills. After passing quickly through the telecommunications industry—working with value-added services and mobile applications—he got the opportunity to join the Santiago studio of DeNA, one of the world's largest mobile video game companies.

In 2013, Angelo was asked to move to Vancouver, Canada, to become a lead software engineer, where he helped build the fledgling Canadian studio and, in particular, championed Unity 3D, paving the way for other teams' adoption and use.

He's known for getting things done by shooting first and asking questions later. When he is not coding and pushing content to GitHub, you'll find him playing table tennis with his friends or running along the sea wall. To know more about him, visit his website at http://angelotadres.com/.

This book is dedicated to my daughter, Antonia Tadres, and my wife, María Jose Arcos, the person whom I love and who has always supported me in all my crazy projects, including the time when I said "You know what? I want to write a book!"

Thanks to my mom; dad; my whole family; and my friends Jorge Bravo and Vartan Ishanoglu for always being there to push me whenever I doubted myself.

I would also like to say thanks to all the people who work at DeNA Studios Canada for making the past 2 years the most amazing ones of my life.

Finally, I would like to thank the Packt Publishing staff for their assistance through the process and the technical reviewers for their feedback, especially Riddhi Tuljapurkar and Fernando Matarrubia.

About the Reviewers

J. Alberto Gandullo Avila graduated from the University of Seville after a 5-year course in computer science (BA/MA). After this, he worked in Seville as a software developer in the field of enterprise management tools for more than 3 years. However, he always liked other fields such as computer graphics and mobile software more, so he began to self-train in the development of mobile apps and mobile games, specifically in the new technology of augmented reality; this was his first contact with the Unity game engine. Thanks to his proficiency in this field, in 2013, he was hired in London (UK) by a small start-up dedicated to the development of educational video games for mobile devices based on augmented reality. At this stage, he became an expert in developing games using technologies such as C# and Unity. After one and a half years in London, Alberto was hired in Bangkok (Thailand) by a company dedicated to developing F2P games for mobile devices.

Jeremy Jones is a game developer who graduated from Neumont University and has a passion for making robust systems within games. He has created many games and several tools in his own game engine and Unity. In his free time, he likes to go hiking, work out, and draw road designs.

> I would like to thank my friends at Neumont University for their support and my family on the East Coast for always believing in me.

Noah Johnson is a technical artist currently working at InContext Solutions. He specializes in pipeline tools and extensions between Unity, Maya, and standalone Python apps. He teaches game engine scripting courses as an adjunct professor at Columbia College Chicago and is currently working on an independent Unreal 4 horror game project. His background in game system scripting and 3D asset creation has dovetailed into a skill set that focuses on tools that make content creation simpler and easier to iterate.

Fernando Matarrubia is a passionate traveler and game maker. He completed his bachelor's degree in computer engineering, for which he was required to travel between three cities and two countries. After that, he got a master's degree in video game development from the Complutense University of Madrid. He has been working with Unity for almost 6 years and loves to create fun pieces of entertainment. He has participated in several titles for platforms such as PS3, PC, Mac, and mobile devices.

Fernando is currently living with his wife and working as a software engineer in the San Francisco Bay Area.

Hugo Ruivo is a self-taught game programmer, who is currently making games for both the mobile and desktop platforms. Alongside games, he also creates tools that help him and his team in the making of their products. He even launched one of his own tools for Unity 3D on the marketplace, Achievement Service Manager.

Ever since he found out how games were made, he couldn't stop learning about the many disciplines of game development, trying to make his own engine, learning new frameworks and technologies, and specializing in some of the best game engines in the industry, such as Unity 3D and UE4.

I would like to thank to my brother and my best friends, who have always given me the inspiration and strength to keep moving forward. I would also like to thank Packt Publishing and Angelo Tadres for the opportunity to contribute to this book and, at some point, to be able to help others learn the same way as I have been learning.

Eric Spevacek, once an independent developer in Chicago, is now an industry technical artist based out of Southern California. His holistic approach to game development and independent experience have helped guide and shape his work in tool development. At work, he is responsible for the creation and maintenance of content creation tools with an emphasis on user experience and streamlined modern workflows. The current trends of accessible commercial game engines and their long-term impact on the industry excite him.

www.PacktPub.com

Support files, eBooks, discount offers, and more

For support files and downloads related to your book, please visit www.PacktPub.com.

Did you know that Packt offers eBook versions of every book published, with PDF and ePub files available? You can upgrade to the eBook version at www.PacktPub.com and as a print book customer, you are entitled to a discount on the eBook copy. Get in touch with us at service@packtpub.com for more details.

At www.PacktPub.com, you can also read a collection of free technical articles, sign up for a range of free newsletters and receive exclusive discounts and offers on Packt books and eBooks.

https://www2.packtpub.com/books/subscription/packtlib

Do you need instant solutions to your IT questions? PacktLib is Packt's online digital book library. Here, you can search, access, and read Packt's entire library of books.

Why subscribe?

- Fully searchable across every book published by Packt
- Copy and paste, print, and bookmark content
- On demand and accessible via a web browser

Free access for Packt account holders

If you have an account with Packt at www.PacktPub.com, you can use this to access PacktLib today and view 9 entirely free books. Simply use your login credentials for immediate access.

Table of Contents

Preface

Unity is a development platform for creating multiplatform 3D and 2D video games, which is adopted by several studios and indie developers who are looking for something simple, flexible, and powerful. One of its most interesting features is the extensible editor, allowing you to make Unity work for your video game using editor scripting.

If you are looking for a book that will show you how to deal with tasks that are beyond the implementation of Gameplay and are more related to automating and simplifying the creation of content, such as the assets that require a special configuration to make them usable in your levels, and how to enable pipelines to consume and create artifacts used by your video game, then this book is for you.

While improving the workflow of *Run & Jump*, a 2D platformer videogame, you will learn all the basics of editor scripting, creating an ad hoc tool that works as a level editor, customizing the way Unity imports assets, and getting control over the build creation process. As a bonus, you will also learn how to share the tools created inside your team or sell them at the Asset Store.

By the end of this book, you will be able to extend all the concepts that you learned to build your own tools and customize the Unity editor in future video game projects with confidence.

You can consider this as an entry point to make your development workflow easier.

Enjoy!

What this book covers

Chapter 1, Getting Started with Editor Scripting, introduces you to Unity editor scripting and explains why this is useful to improve the development workflow. In this chapter, the video game, *Run & Jump*, which is used as a base for this book is presented.

Chapter 2, Using Gizmos in the Scene View, explains how to use gizmos to display debug information in the Scene View. Here, we implement a grid with gizmos to be used as guides in the level editor.

Chapter 3, Creating Custom Inspectors, discusses how to improve the way the Unity components and scripts are presented in the inspector window, creating custom inspectors and using property and decorator drawers. In addition to the this, you will learn how to start adding and using the editor GUI components. Here we go through the process of making a custom inspector for the class responsible for the level logic in *Run & Jump*.

Chapter 4, Creating Editor Windows, covers how to create an editor window to present information and interact with features in a custom tool. Using some of the editor GUI skills developed in the last chapter, we create a *Palette* window, which is a quick and visual way to access the prefabs used as building pieces for the video game levels, grouping them by categories.

Chapter 5, Customizing the Scene View, dives into how to add the editor GUI components directly to the Scene View and capture specific events to expand their capabilities. Step by step, we add GUI components to enable and disable different modes we are going to implement on the level editor, like View, Paint, Edit and Erase, changing the way how the user interacts with the tool.

Chapter 6, Changing the Look and Feel of the Editor with GUI Styles and GUI Skins, explains how to change the look and feel of the Unity editor custom tools. Here we finish the level editor investing our time modifying the appearance of it.

Chapter 7, Saving Data in a Persistent Way with Scriptable Objects, describes how to save data in Unity and manipulate it as a reusable asset using scriptable objects. We walk through the process of reallocate certain properties from the class responsible for the level logic to a scriptable object class, making them reusable across levels.

Chapter 8, Controlling the Import Pipeline Using Asset Postprocessor Scripts, demonstrates how to improve and control the importing pipeline using Asset Postprocessor scripts. We work in automating the process of changing the import settings of the assets imported to the project to make them usable by the video game in an easy way.

Chapter 9, Improving the Build Pipeline, discusses how to automate and improve the build creation pipeline modifying the Unity player settings through code and calling scripts outside Unity. Here, we create a basic build pipeline for Run & Jump that publishes the mobile version of it in a distribution platform called AppBlade.

Chapter 10, Distributing Your Tools, concludes this book by showing how to use Unity packages and Git submodules for custom tools distribution, suitable for sharing inside a team, and how to sell content on the Asset Store.

What you need for this book

To follow this book, you will need to download a copy of Unity available at `https://unity3d.com/get-unity`.

You can use any version of Unity from version 5.0, but we recommend the latest 5.x version, which at the time of writing this is version 5.1.2 (all screenshots have been updated to this version). Don't worry about the kind of license you have, the examples will work with the Personal and Professional Edition.

While working with this book, we will use as base project the video game *Run & Jump*, available at `https://github.com/angelotadres/RunAndJump`.

You must have the *Run & Jump* project in order to test the code in this book.

Who this book is for

This book is for anyone who has basic knowledge of Unity programming using C# and wants to learn how to extend and create custom tools using Unity Editor Scripting to improve the development workflow and make video game development easier.

Conventions

In this book, you will find a number of text styles that distinguish between different kinds of information. Here are some examples of these styles and an explanation of their meaning.

Code words in text, database table names, folder names, filenames, file extensions, pathnames, dummy URLs, user input, and Twitter handles are shown as follows: "Create a script called `LevelInspector.cs` inside the folder `Editor`"

A block of code is set as follows:

```
public override void OnInspectorGUI() {
    DrawLevelDataGUI();
    DrawLevelSizeGUI();
}
```

When we wish to draw your attention to a particular part of a code block, the relevant lines or items are set in bold:

```
public override void OnInspectorGUI() {
    DrawLevelDataGUI();
    DrawLevelSizeGUI();
}
```

Any command-line input or output is written as follows:

```
$ git submodule update
```

New terms and **important words** are shown in bold. Words that you see on the screen, for example, in menus or dialog boxes, appear in the text like this: "Select the category **Misc** and then click on the **Sign** piece"

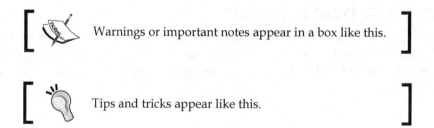

Warnings or important notes appear in a box like this.

Tips and tricks appear like this.

Reader feedback

Feedback from our readers is always welcome. Let us know what you think about this book—what you liked or disliked. Reader feedback is important for us as it helps us develop titles that you will really get the most out of.

To send us general feedback, simply e-mail feedback@packtpub.com, and mention the book's title in the subject of your message.

If there is a topic that you have expertise in and you are interested in either writing or contributing to a book, see our author guide at www.packtpub.com/authors.

Customer support

Now that you are the proud owner of a Packt book, we have a number of things to help you to get the most from your purchase.

Downloading the example code

You can download the example code files from your account at http://www.packtpub.com for all the Packt Publishing books you have purchased. If you purchased this book elsewhere, you can visit http://www.packtpub.com/support and register to have the files e-mailed directly to you.

Errata

Although we have taken every care to ensure the accuracy of our content, mistakes do happen. If you find a mistake in one of our books—maybe a mistake in the text or the code—we would be grateful if you could report this to us. By doing so, you can save other readers from frustration and help us improve subsequent versions of this book. If you find any errata, please report them by visiting http://www.packtpub.com/submit-errata, selecting your book, clicking on the **Errata Submission Form** link, and entering the details of your errata. Once your errata are verified, your submission will be accepted and the errata will be uploaded to our website or added to any list of existing errata under the Errata section of that title.

To view the previously submitted errata, go to https://www.packtpub.com/books/content/support and enter the name of the book in the search field. The required information will appear under the **Errata** section.

Piracy

Piracy of copyrighted material on the Internet is an ongoing problem across all media. At Packt, we take the protection of our copyright and licenses very seriously. If you come across any illegal copies of our works in any form on the Internet, please provide us with the location address or website name immediately so that we can pursue a remedy.

Please contact us at copyright@packtpub.com with a link to the suspected pirated material.

We appreciate your help in protecting our authors and our ability to bring you valuable content.

Questions

If you have a problem with any aspect of this book, you can contact us at questions@packtpub.com, and we will do our best to address the problem.

1
Getting Started with Editor Scripting

Unity is a powerful engine that enables creative people like you to build video games in different platforms.

After developing a few projects on it, you will realize that each of these could have been a better experience if you'd had a tool at that time to help you in the creation of content for your video game or in the automation of all those manual repetitive tasks that always end up generating a problem at the worst moment just because of Murphy's Law.

To create tools based on your video game requirements, Unity provides an **editor scripting API** to do it in a quick and fully integrated way. However, the documentation available for building such tools by yourself is not the best.

The main aim of this book is to give you a tour of some of the most important topics about editor scripting . We are going to explore its API when at the same time we implement custom tools to improve the development workflow in *Run & Jump*, a 2D platformer video game.

In this chapter, we will cover the following topics:

- Basics of editor scripting
- *Run & Jump* presentation and definition of the scope of the custom tools

Overview

Probably, at this point, you are familiar with the basic concepts of Unity and we can safely assume that you know how to create a small video game from scratch without too many complications. You know, for projects of this size, almost everything is always under control and nothing takes too much time to be done. Basically, it is like a little paradise in the video game developer's land.

However, when the project starts increasing in size in terms of complexity, you will notice that certain tasks are repetitive or subject to error, generating a considerable amount of effort and waste of time. For example, the mechanics of your video game are quite unique and it is hard for the level designers to create content on time and without errors. This is because Unity, or the available third-party tool you use, doesn't satisfy all the required functionalities.

Sometimes, because you have more people working on the project, the lack of a mechanism to encourage people to follow standards makes your video game crash constantly.

In the same scenario, imagine that your project also requires a lot of art assets, so artists constantly add these to Unity. The problem appears later when one of the developers needs to constantly check whether the settings of these assets are configured properly to make these look right in the final build, consuming development time.

Finally, your project will be available on several platforms. However, owing to the specific characteristics of your video game, every time you make a production build, you must check whether all the settings are okay. You also need to check whether you removed all the cheat menus used by your testers and that the correct assets are loaded into each because you are preparing a trial version. Managing this becomes a huge task!

To solve all these issues, Unity provides an editor scripting API. Using this we can do the following tasks:

- Modify how the Unity editor behaves, triggering our code with specific events
- Improve the workflow assistance with a custom GUI that seamlessly integrates with the Unity editor GUI
- Automate repetitive tasks by accessing the Unity editor's main functionalities

Understating how to use the editor scripting API to create editor scripts in your project will allow you to make Unity work for your video game and boost the productivity of the video game development.

Editor scripting basics

It's time to go hands on in the creation of editor scripts so in this section we are going to explore how to start them off.

What is an editor script?

An **editor script** is any piece of code that uses methods from the **UnityEditor** namespace, and its principal objective is to create or modify functionalities in the Unity editor.

To see this working, let's start with a basic example. Create a new project in Unity and then a new script called HelloWorld.cs. Don't worry about where to place the script, we'll talk about that in a bit. Copy the following code:

```
using UnityEngine;
using UnityEditor;

public class HelloWorld {

    [MenuItem ("GameObject/Create HelloWorld")]
    private static void CreateHelloWorldGameObject () {
        if(EditorUtility.DisplayDialog(
            "Hello World",
            "Do you really want to do this?",
            "Create",
            "Cancel")) {
            new GameObject("HelloWorld");
        }
    }
}
```

Wait for the compiler to finish and then go to the Unity editor menu and click on **GameObject**. At the end of the menu, you will see an item called **Create HelloWorld**, as shown in the following screenshot:

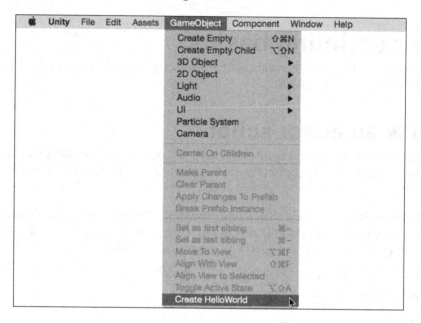

Click on this item, then a dialog window asks whether you really want to create this game object:

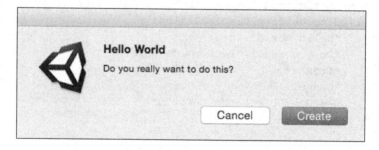

After clicking on **Create**, a new game object with the name **HelloWorld** is added to the current scene. You can check this in the **Hierarchy** window:

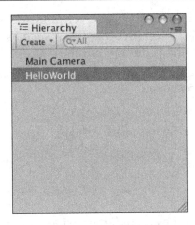

You created your first editor script using two things:

- A `MenuItem` attribute to add menu items to the Unity editor menu.
- A `DisplayDialog` method, part of the `EditorUtility` class, to show a custom model popup.

Don't worry, we will discuss these in depth later in this book. For now, we are going to move forward and discuss something very important in the creation of editor scripts: the `Editor` folder.

The Editor folder

The `Editor` folder is one of the special folders Unity has, just like the `Resources` or `Plugins` folders.

Like the Unity documentation says, all scripts inside a folder with the name *Editor* will be treated as editor scripts rather than runtime scripts related to your video game. Also, you can have more than one Editor folder in your project at once if you want.

To learn more about other special folders in Unity, visit `http://docs.unity3d.com/Manual/SpecialFolders.html`.

If you have at least one `Editor` folder with a script inside, you will see something like the following in MonoDevelop (in other IDEs, such as Visual Studio or Xamarin, you may see something slightly different, but the concept is the same):

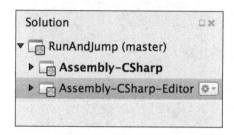

Two different assemblies will be created: the first assembly, **Assembly-CSharp**, is for your video game scripts and the second assembly, **Assembly-CSharp-Editor**, is for your editor scripts. This means that the editor scripts will not be included in your final video game build.

So, what is the problem with `HelloWorld.cs`? Well, right now it's not inside an `Editor` folder, so if you try to build a video game with that script included, the build process will fail because Unity won't be able to find the namespace named UnityEditor:

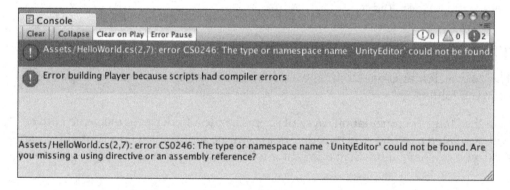

Most of the editor scripts that we will discuss in this book, like **custom inspectors** in *Chapter 3, Creating Custom Inspectors*, or **editor windows** in *Chapter 4, Creating Editor Windows* require being saved inside an Editor folder in order to work. However, in some situations, it is possible to achieve this without using the `Editor` folder.

Let's fix the original `HelloWorld.cs` file to work outside an `Editor` folder. In this case, we must tell the compiler to not include the editor-related code if we are making a video game build.

To achieve this, we will use the preprocessor directives #if and #endif with the conditional compilation symbol UNITY_EDITOR. Using both together, we can tell the compiler to exclude a block of code when we create a video game build.

Update HelloWorld.cs as follows:

```
using UnityEngine;
#if UNITY_EDITOR
using UnityEditor;
#endif
public class HelloWorld {

    #if UNITY_EDITOR
    [MenuItem ("GameObject/Create HelloWorld")]
    private static void CreateHelloWorldGameObject () {
        if(EditorUtility.DisplayDialog(
            "Hello World",
            "Do you really want to do this?",
            "Create",
            "Cancel")) {
            new GameObject("HelloWorld");
        }
    }
    #endif

    // Add your video game code here
}
```

If you feel a little overwhelmed, just keep in mind that the last script example is an exception, and as a guideline, all the editor scripts must be inside an Editor folder. to keep everything organized and working

Introducing Run & Jump

Run & Jump is a 2D platformer video game created for this book to serve as a base for our editor scripting experiments. In this section, we will talk about the video game and what kind of things we want to achieve.

Keep in mind that it is not important to understand in detail how *Run & Jump* is implemented. It's enough just to understand the workflows associated with the content creation of this video game.

Playing the video game

In this video game, the player takes control of *Timmy*, a guy who likes to collect coins and invests his time searching for hidden treasures. On his journey, he needs to avoid obstacles and enemies to reach the finale of each level and win. You can see how the video game looks in the following screenshots:

To play the video game, you will have to clone or download the project from `https://github.com/angelotadres/RunAndJump` in GitHub.

When you are ready, open the project in Unity. You will see the following folder structure in the **Project** browser:

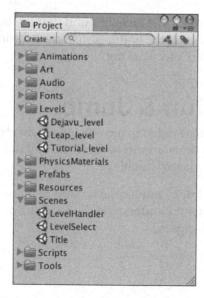

To test the game, open the scene **Title** inside the **Scenes** folder and then press the **Play** button in the Unity toolbar:

To control *Timmy*, use the left and right arrows on your keyboard. Pressing the space bar makes him jump, and pressing it again while he is in the air makes him perform a double jump.

Currently, there are three levels implemented for this video game to test its functionality. In the next section, you will learn how to add more levels.

Creating a new level

In this video game, each level is a Unity scene inside the folder `Levels`. When you start playing *Run & Jump* and then select a specific level, the video game call the `LevelHandler` scene and this starts the script `LevelHandlerScene.cs`.

This scene has all the GUI necessary for the level, and the script is responsible for the game's status detection (playing, paused, and so on), when the player wins or loses, and loading of the specific level scene using the method `Application.LoadLevelAdditive`.

 Unlike `LoadLevel`, `LoadLevelAdditive` does not destroy objects in the current scene. Objects from the new scene are added over the current one.

Each level scene is composed of several prefabs. We will refer to these in the rest of the book as *level pieces prefabs*.

Navigate to `Prefabs | LevelPieces` to check the available level piece prefabs. The following table contains a description of each one:

Level Piece	Description
	Timmy (`Player.prefab`): You control this character in the game. Timmy's abilities are run, jump and double jump. There's nothing to envy about the Italian plumber.
	Angry Blob (`EnemyAngryBlob.prefab`): This character moves over platforms from one side to the other with an angry face. You don't like him and he doesn't like you so don't touch him or you will lose a life!
	Coins (`InteractiveCoin.prefab`): It is not a real platform video game without something to collect. Coins are one of the collectibles, and when you pick one, your score increases by 100 points.
	Treasure (`InteractiveTreasure.prefab`): Usually, this collectable is well hidden in order to motivate the player to explore the level. When you pick one, your score increases by 1,000 points.
	Sign (`InteractiveSign.prefab`): This will display a message on the screen when the player is around the sign board. The sign is used to give the player hints or miscellaneous information about the current level.

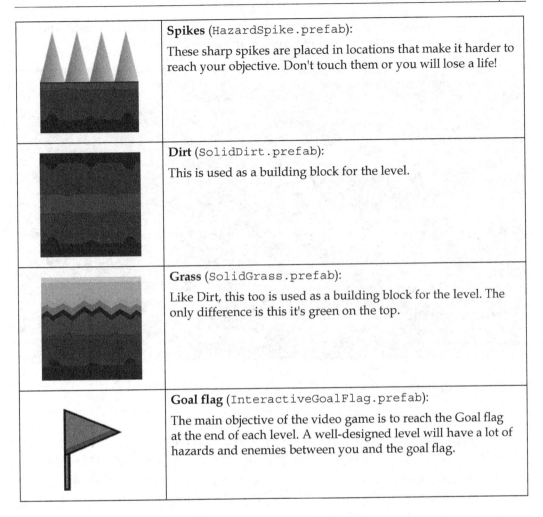

	Spikes (`HazardSpike.prefab`): These sharp spikes are placed in locations that make it harder to reach your objective. Don't touch them or you will lose a life!
	Dirt (`SolidDirt.prefab`): This is used as a building block for the level.
	Grass (`SolidGrass.prefab`): Like Dirt, this too is used as a building block for the level. The only difference is this it's green on the top.
	Goal flag (`InteractiveGoalFlag.prefab`): The main objective of the video game is to reach the Goal flag at the end of each level. A well-designed level will have a lot of hazards and enemies between you and the goal flag.

To get a better understating of what is involved in creating levels, let's create a new one. The goal is to copy the following level (or at least try to do so):

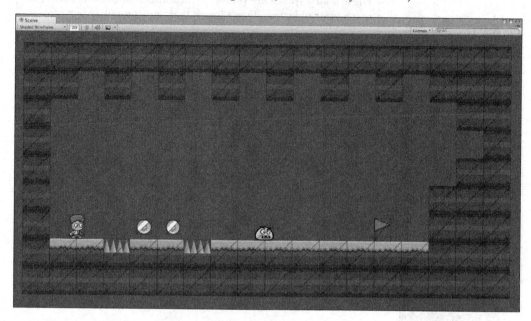

For this, you need to perform the following steps:

1. Create a new scene and remove the default camera.

2. Add a new **Game Object** to the scene and attach the `level.cs` script located in `Scripts | Level`. This script contains the base to make our level work.

3. Navigate to `Prefabs | LevelPieces` and clone the prefabs in the scene until you complete creating the level. All the prefabs must be nested inside the game object you created earlier.

4. When you are done, click again on the root game object. If you check the **Inspector** window, you will see the following:

Here, you will be able to adjust the properties of the level, such as the maximum time taken to beat the level and get the score bonus, **Gravity**, **Bgm** (background music), and **Background**. You can play with these values: for the Bgm, you can grab an audio clip from the folder `Audio/Bgm`; and for the background, you can grab a sprite from `Art/Bg`.

5. As soon you finish, save the scene inside the folder `Levels` with the name `MyLevel_level`.

 To align the prefabs among themselves, select the **Transform** tool and press and hold the *V* key to activate the **Vertex-Snapping mode**.

Run & Jump comes with a custom tool that allows you to set up the order and the name of the levels and also add these to the **Scenes in Build** list automatically. We must use this in order of make our level usable by the video game (one of the requirements is to include the suffix `_level` in the name of the scene).

In the Unity editor menu, navigate to **Tools | Level Packager | Show Levels Package**:

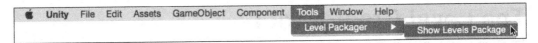

This will display the following in the **Inspector** window:

Currently, there are only three levels listed, so click on the **+** icon to create a new item in the list. Now, add the scene you created in right column and add the string **My Level** in the left column. This will add your level as the fourth one.

Save the changes by clicking on the **Commit Levels** button.

To check the scene you created, open the scene **Title** inside the **Scenes** folder, and then click on the **Play** button to run the video game:

Now you know the necessary amount of effort it takes to create a level for this game; so let's make this level creation process the first thing to improve.

The Level Creator tool

Imagine a scenario where you are responsible for generating several levels for *Run & Jump*. You know this task is time consuming, and copying and pasting prefabs to place them in the right position is not the most efficient way to achieve this.

Basically, most of the 2D level editors use a **Canvas/Brush** metaphor to design the user interaction. This means the level scene is your canvas and using the mouse cursor as a brush, you paint over it level prefab instances.

Taking this in to consideration, the first thing we will create is a tool called **Level Creator** to make this process easier using the Canvas/Brush metaphor, and of course, in the process, we will cover several editor scripting topics.

The features of the Level Creator are as follows:

- Automates the creation of a scene capable of being used as a level. This means that you can generate a scene with a game object, and the level script attached to it, with just a simple click.
- Displays a grid on the **Scene View** option to be used as a reference. All the level piece prefabs will snap to this grid by default.
- Controls and validates how the properties of the level script are changed.
- Improves the visibility of the available level pieces prefabs by creating a Palette window to show a preview. This classifies the prefabs by their category.
- Implements the Canvas/Brush metaphor allowing fourt modes: view, paint, edit, and erase level pieces prefabs.
- Customizes the look and feel of the tool to improve its own appearance.

For now, let's focus on automating the creation of a scene capable to be used as a level.

As you notice, *Run & Jump* is fully playable at it is but we are going to make a few improvements in its implementation to achieve a seamless integration with the Level Creator tool. Is because of that, all the current levels aren't be editable by the tool.

All the design decisions in this book were taken in order to make easy to understand the code related to editor scripting.

Defining the chapter goals

In the rest of this chapter, we will work on the first scripts of the **Level Creator** tool in order to automate the creation of a scene capable to be used as a level.

The goals here are:

- Create a new Unity scene by code
- Add a game object with the level script attached to it to the scene by code
- Create a menu item to trigger the creation of a scene capable to be used as a level in the Unity editor menu

Preparing the environment

We need to create a few folders to keep our development organized. Remember, for this entire book, we are working on the *Run & Jump* project.

You will find a folder called **Tools** in the root of the project. Right now this folder has one inside with the scripts of the tool we used to add our levels to the game.

Inside the **Tools** folder, create a new folder called **LevelCreator** and then match the folder structure, as shown in the following screenshot:

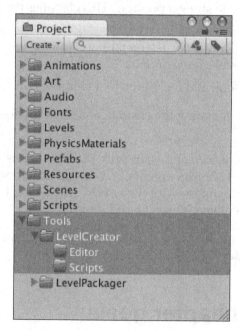

This folder structure is just a suggestion, but you must always consider creating a root folder for your custom tools.

Performing automation

As we were saying, we want to create a scene capable to be used as a level, but instead doing this manually in Unity, we are going to achieve the same using code.

We are going to implement a few methods to do this. Inside the folder `Tools/LevelCreator/Editor`, create a new script called `EditorUtils.cs` and add the following code:

```csharp
using UnityEngine;
using UnityEditor;
using System.Collections.Generic;

namespace RunAndJump.LevelCreator {
  public static class EditorUtils {

    // Creates a new scene
    public static void NewScene () {
      EditorApplication.SaveCurrentSceneIfUserWantsTo ();
      EditorApplication.NewScene ();
    }

    // Remove all the elements of the scene
    public static void CleanScene () {
      GameObject[] allObjects = Object.FindObjectsOfType<GameObject>
();
      foreach (GameObject go in allObjects) {
        GameObject.DestroyImmediate (go);
      }
    }

    // Creates a new scene capable to be used as a level
    public static void NewLevel () {
      NewScene ();
      CleanScene ();
      GameObject levelGO = new GameObject ("Level");
      levelGO.transform.position = Vector3.zero;
      levelGO.AddComponent<Level> ();
    }
  }
}
```

The NewLevel method is the one that executes all the work using the help of the following two methods:

- NewScene: This creates a new scene, but before doing that, asks whether we want to save the scene that is currently open. All this is done using EditorApplication, a static class with several methods to know the state of the editor (playing, paused, compiling, and so on) and create, save, or load scenes and projects.

- CleanScene: This removes all the elements of the scene. Remember the camera created by default with each scene in Unity? Well, this method is going to take care of that using the DestroyImmediate method. This is similar to the common Destroy method but this works in an Editor context.

To learn more about the EditorApplication class, visit http:// docs.unity3d.com/ScriptReference/EditorApplication. html.

In order to avoid class name conflicts, it's always a good idea to use namespaces. In this project, all the video game classes are in the RunAndJump namespace and the Level Creator classes are in the LevelCreator.RunAndJump namespace.

Similar to the HelloWorld example we created at the beginning of this chapter, we need to make the NewLevel method accessible through the Unity editor menu using the MenuItem attribute.

Inside the folder Tools/LevelCreator/Editor, create a new script called MenuItems.cs. We will use this to add all the future menu items that the tool requires; for now, add the following code:

```csharp
using UnityEngine;
using UnityEditor;

namespace RunAndJump.LevelCreator {
  public static class MenuItems {

      [MenuItem ("Tools/Level Creator/New Level Scene")]
      private static void NewLevel () {
          EditorUtils.NewLevel ();
      }
    }
}
```

Now, the `NewLevel` method will be available when you navigate to **Tools | Level Creator | New Level Scene**. Save all the scripts changes and for Unity to compile, then click on **New Level Scene**:

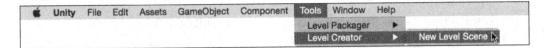

A dialog window will ask you whether you want to save the current changes of the scene (if this one has modifications):

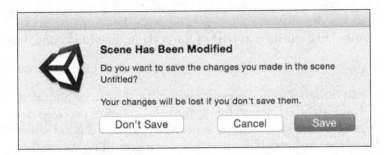

After this, a new scene will be created with the game object containing the level script:

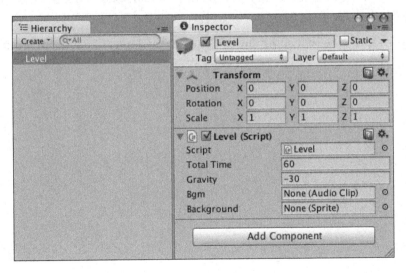

Congratulations! We have the starting point for the Level Creator tool creating a level scene with just one click!

Summary

In this chapter, we introduced you to the editor scripting API and also the project that we will use in this book.

With editor scripts, we were able to customize how Unity works and customize the workflow based on our specific requirements.

When you work with editor scripts, remember to use the `UnityEditor` namespace and save the scripts inside a folder with the name `Editor`.

If for some reason you must use the editor scripting API outside an `Editor` folder, remember to use the directives `#if` and `#endif` with the `UNITY_EDITOR` conditional compilation symbol to exclude that part of the code in the video game build.

If you plan to create a custom tool in your project, always consider these two things:

- When you design a tool, always consider the user for whom you are building the tool and involve them in the design and creation process. If your tool requires a custom GUI, creating mockups is always a good alternative to get an idea of the final result. Remember, there is nothing worse than a tool that is not easy to use and doesn't solve the specific problem.

- Always evaluate the cost of creating the tool and the time you want to invest in that. Ensure that the time and resources you spend creating the tool itself to save more time and resources later during development.

In the next chapter, we will continue working on the Level Creator, integrating the use of gizmos to display a grid meant to be used as guides in our tool.

2
Using Gizmos in the Scene View

When you are working on a video game and you need to debug features, it's very helpful to have a visual representation of certain structures you are using in the code. For example, imagine that you have a set of waypoints to model the movement of a **Non Playable Character** (**NPC**) in your video game. If it is possible for you to see the waypoints, it will be easier for you to make tweaks and readjust the movement paths.

Thankfully, in Unity there's a class called **Gizmos** that allow us to add visual aids to the **Scene View** in an easy way.

Here, you will learn about the Gizmos class and how to use this to create a visual grid that will help level designers position the level piece prefabs with more control in the level.

In this chapter we will cover the following topics:

- The `OnDrawGizmos` and `OnDrawGizmosSelected` methods
- The `DrawGizmo` attribute
- The Gizmos class API

Overview

In Unity, a gizmo is a visual aid rendered in Unity's **Scene View** to help us in the development process. Several components in Unity use gizmos to tell the developers where in the 3D world these are located.

Take a look at the following screenshot. The two icons, the movie camera and the light bulb, are gizmos that indicate the game object position of the camera and the point light components, respectively.

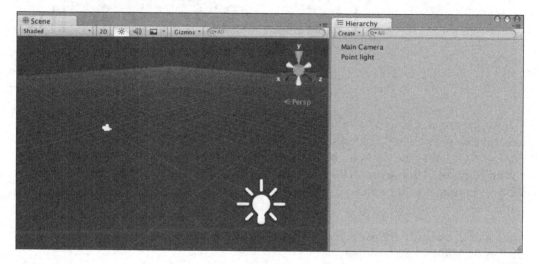

You can do the same with a specific game object if you click on the cube icon in their inspector pane:

Here you have three options to choose:

- Use a label
- Use a built-in icon
- Use a custom icon made with any image located inside your project

You will see the following three results, respectively, in the **Scene View**:

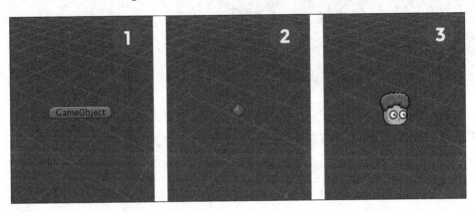

Any of these gizmos will be attached to the game object and will persist in the scene and in any prefab containing this game object.

All these examples use the Unity editor to do the required setup, but there is an additional way in which gizmos can be created, allowing greater flexibility due to the use of parameters related to our game logic. This is achieved through code using the Gizmos class.

Defining the chapter goals

In this chapter, we will start exploring the many alternatives we have for adding gizmos to Unity and then finish with the implementation of a visual grid for positioning the level piece prefabs, setting the boundaries for our level in this way.

The goals here are:

- Exploring how to add gizmos through code
- Defining the size of the level in terms of columns and rows
- Rendering a grid using gizmos based on the size of the level
- Implementing a snap to grid feature using the level piece prefabs

The final result that we will achieve looks like this:

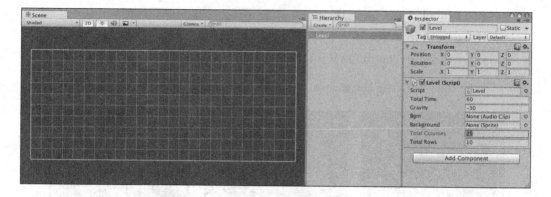

Creating gizmos through code

We explored how to add simple gizmos through the Unity editor. This section will cover how to properly implement the OnDrawGizmos and OnDrawGizmosSelected methods to achieve a similar but more flexible solution.

> All the scripts in this section are examples, and are not meant to be used in the Level Creator tool.

The OnDrawGizmos and OnDrawGizmosSelected methods

To get started, in a new project, create a script called GizmoExample.cs. We will use this as a guinea pig for our first gizmos experiments (don't worry, the script is not going to suffer too much!)

Write the following code in GizmoExample.cs:

```
using UnityEngine;
public class GizmoExample : MonoBehaviour {
        private void OnDrawGizmos() {
        }
}
```

When you implement the OnDrawGizmos method, you can add gizmos that always drawn in the **Scene View** and also allows the possibility to be selected with a click.

In this case, the method is empty. However, if you come back to Unity and wait for the compiler to end, you'll find that the class **GizmoExample** is listed in the **Gizmos** dropdown on the **Scene View**:

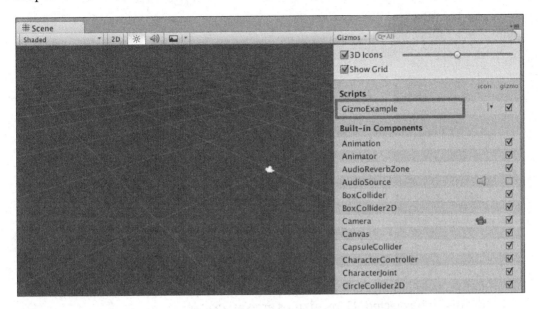

The **Gizmos** dropdown allows you to change the way gizmos are displayed in the **Scene View**. At the top of the dropdown, you can change the scale size that gizmos are drawn at; next to that, you will see a list of the available gizmos. To turn gizmos on or off, simply click on the checkbox to hide or show the gizmo itself.

If you select the column icon associated with **GizmoExample**, you will get the same kind of results we saw when we clicked on the cube icon in the inspector. Here, again, you can choose between using a label, a built-in icon, or a custom icon. For now, just choose a label.

 Changing the icon in the **Gizmos** dropdown will also change the icon used to represent the script in the **Project** browser and the inspector.

As soon you add the `GizmoExample.cs` script to a new game object in the scene, a gizmo label with the name of the game object will be displayed in the **Scene View**.

 The `OnDrawGizmos` method is not called if the component collapses in the **inspector** window.

We explored a simple way to make our script visible to Unity, but there are more powerful things to explore. Remove the icon from the **Gizmos** dropdown and update the GizmoExample.cs script as follows:

```
using UnityEngine;

public class GizmoExample : MonoBehaviour {

    private void OnDrawGizmos () {
        Gizmos.color = Color.white;
        Gizmos.DrawCube (
            transform.position, Vector3.one);
    }

    private void OnDrawGizmosSelected () {
        Gizmos.color = Color.red;
        Gizmos.DrawWireCube (
            transform.position, Vector3.one);
    }
}
```

We added a new method, OnDrawGizmosSelected. Implement this to draw gizmos only if the object is selected. Here, gizmos aren't pickable.

Inside the OnDrawGizmos and OnDrawGizmosSelected methods, we made use of the Gizmos class to draw gizmos. Now, you should see a solid cube in the position of the game object with the GizmoExample.cs script attached, and then a solid cube with a color outline when this game object is selected:

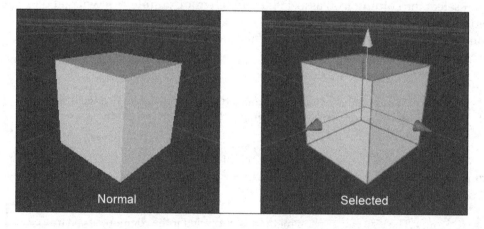

At this point, you may have noticed that the Gizmos class is part of the `UnityEngine` namespace instead of the `UnityEditor` namespace. This means you can use it in your `MonoBehaviour` class directly if you have the method `OnDrawGizmos` or `OnDrawGizmosSelected` implemented.

 Take into consideration that these methods are called in an Editor context and will not be available in your final video game.

Adding gizmos using the DrawGizmo attribute

The `DrawGizmo` attribute allows you to display gizmos using a separated class from the original `MonoBehaviour` class and without using the `OnDrawGizmos` or `OnDrawGizmosSelected` method explicitly.

Here, we will need two scripts. The first one, called `TargetExample.cs`, is the `MonoBehaviour` class we want to add the gizmo; and the second one, called `DrawGizmoExample.cs` is a script that implements the gizmo.

Let's start creating the script `TargetExample.cs` in a new project:

```
using UnityEngine;

public class TargetExample : MonoBehaviour {

}
```

As we can see, no gizmo logic was added here. Because the `DrawGizmo` attribute is part of the `UnityEditor` namespace, we will create the `DrawGizmoExample.cs` script inside an `Editor` folder. For this, add the following code:

```
using UnityEngine;
using UnityEditor;

public class DrawGizmoExample {

    // This emulates OnDrawGizmos
    [DrawGizmo(GizmoType.NotInSelectionHierarchy |
            GizmoType.InSelectionHierarchy |
            GizmoType.Selected |
            GizmoType.Active |
            GizmoType.Pickable)]
    private static void MyCustomOnDrawGizmos(
```

```
        TargetExample targetExample, GizmoType gizmoType) {
        Gizmos.color = Color.white;
        Gizmos.DrawCube(
            targetExample.transform.position, Vector3.one);
    }
}
```

Save everything you've done so far, and in a new scene, add a game object with `TargetExample.cs` attached. You will see this:

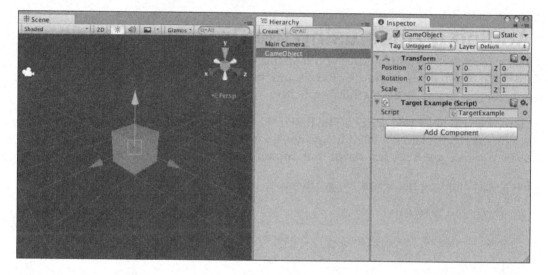

The `TargetExample` class is rendering a gizmos cube similar to the past example, but now the `DrawGizmoExample.cs` , and external editor script, is responsible of that.

Any method meant to be used for render gizmos, in this case, `MyCustomOnDrawGizmos`, must be static and take two parameters: the object for which the gizmo is being drawn, and a `GizmoType` parameter, which indicates the context in which the gizmo is being drawn. Inside this method, you can use the Gizmos class again to add all the gizmos you want.

Then, to make this work, we used the `DrawGizmo` attribute on the method `MyCustomOnDrawGizmos` and passed as parameters the `GizmoType` we want to use. These are flags that specify scenarios in which the gizmos will be rendered and their behavior.

The `GizmoType` method offers five properties you can use:

- `InSelectionHierarchy`: This draws the gizmo if it is selected or it is a child of the selected

- `NotInSelectionHierarchy`: This draws the gizmo if it is not selected and also no parent is selected
- `Selected`: This draws the gizmo if it is selected
- `Active`: This draws the gizmo if it is active (shown in the inspector)
- `Pickable`: The gizmo to be drawn can be picked from the editor

In the case of `MyCustomOnDrawGizmos`, to emulate the behavior of the `OnDrawGizmos` method, we used all the gizmo types available. You can use different combinations to achieve different results, for example, let's try to emulate the behavior of `OnDrawGizmosSelected` creating a method called `MyCustomOnDrawGizmosSelected` inside the `DrawGizmoExample` class:

```
[DrawGizmo(GizmoType.InSelectionHierarchy |
           GizmoType.Active)]
private static void MyCustomOnDrawGizmosSelected(
    TargetExample targetExample, GizmoType gizmoType) {
    Gizmos.color = Color.red;
    Gizmos.DrawWireCube(
        targetExample.transform.position, Vector3.one);
}
```

Save the changes and wait for Unity to compile the scripts, and then you will see the functionality of the original `OnDrawGizmosSelected` method achieved by the `MyCustomOnDrawGizmosSelected` method:

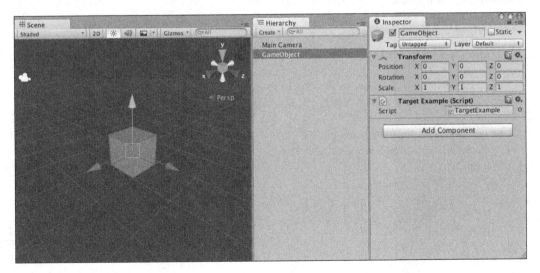

Here, we presented an alternative to rendering gizmos in Unity, but in most cases, using the OnDrawGizmos or OnDrawGizmosSelected method is enough to create visual aids in the **Scene View**.

In which scenarios do you want to use this approach? Well, one instance is if you really want to separate what is related to your video game and what is related to the editor stuff. However, most of the times, this approach would be helpful when you don't have access to the implementation of the specific MonoBehaviour class, so using the method OnDrawGizmos or OnDrawGizmosSelected is not possible.

The Gizmos class

The Gizmos class has all the methods to draw gizmos in the **Scene View** and we will explore these methods in this section. If you want to reproduce the examples that we will work on here, just add the code snippets inside a MonoBehaviour class.

 This section is an extended version of the official documentation about the Gizmos class. If you want to check the original version visit: http://docs.unity3d.com/ScriptReference/ Gizmos.html.

DrawCube

This draws a solid box with center and size.

Example:

```
// Method signature public static void DrawCube(Vector3 center,
Vector3 size);
public Vector3 center = Vector3.zero;
public Vector3 size = Vector3.one;

private void OnDrawGizmos() {
  Gizmos.DrawCube(center, size);
} Result:
```

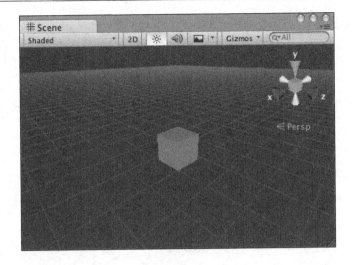

DrawWireCube

This draws a wireframe box with center and size.

Example:

```
// Method signature public static void DrawWireCube(Vector3 center,
Vector3 size);
public Vector3 center = Vector3.zero;
public Vector3 size = Vector3.one;

private void OnDrawGizmos() {
  Gizmos.DrawWireCube(center, size);
} Result:
```

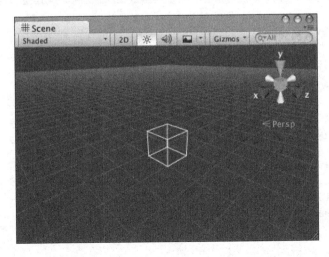

DrawSphere

This draw a solid sphere with center and radius.

Example:

```
// Method signature public static void DrawSphere(Vector3 center,
float radius);
public Vector3 center = Vector3.zero;
public float radius = 1f;

private void OnDrawGizmos() {
  Gizmos.DrawSphere(center, radius);
} Result:
```

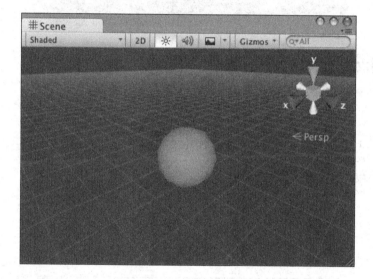

DrawWireSphere

This draws a wireframe sphere with center and radius.

Example:

```
// Method signature public static void DrawWireSphere(Vector3 center,
float radius);
public Vector3 center = Vector3.zero;
public float radius = 1f;

private void OnDrawGizmos() {
  Gizmos.DrawWireSphere(center, radius);
} Result:
```

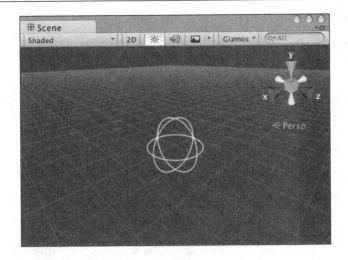

DrawRay

This draws a ray , a line starting at some position and going in some direction. This is a good way to visualize ray casting algorithms when you are unsure what the length or direction of a ray is.

Example:

```
// Method signatures public static void DrawRay(Ray r);
// public static void DrawRay(Vector3 from, Vector3 direction);
public Vector3 from = Vector3.zero;
public Vector3 direction = Vector3.up;

private void OnDrawGizmos() {
  Gizmos.DrawRay(from, direction);
} Result:
```

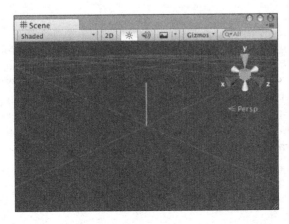

DrawLine

This draws a line.

Example:

```
// Method signature public static void DrawLine(Vector3 from, Vector3
to);
public Vector3 from = new Vector3(1, 0, 0);
public Vector3 to = new Vector3(0, 0, 1);

private void OnDrawGizmos() {
  Gizmos.DrawLine(from, to);
} Result:
```

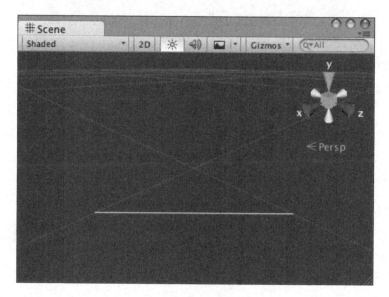

DrawIcon

This draws an icon at the world space Vector3, in Center at the specified position. The icon should be a regular image file, such as a PNG or JPG image, which is to be placed in the Assets/Gizmos folder. Whether or not the icon will be scaled and displayed or hidden is determined in the **Gizmos** dropdown. Using this method instead of the approach we saw at the beginning of this chapter gives you more control over the icons. For example, you can simulate toggle icons to visually represent boolean values in your code.

To make this code work, we previously created a copy of the asset Game/Art/UI/ UI_LivesAvatar.png inside a folder called Gizmos. Note that the icon always faces the **Scene View** camera.

Example:

```
// Method signature public static void DrawIcon(Vector3 center, string
name, bool allowScaling = true);
private void OnDrawGizmos() {
  Gizmos.DrawIcon(
     transform.position, "icon.png");
} Result:
```

DrawGUITexture

This draws the Texture inside the ScreenRect method on the **Scene View** using the XY plane (where the Z coordinate is zero). The values of the texture rectangle are given in scene units.

The optional border values specify an inset from each edge within the rectangle in scene units; the texture is drawn inside the inset rectangle and the edge pixels are repeated outward.

In this example, we pass the reference of the texture as a parameter. You will see that the texture is inverted; this is because the origin of the coordinate system is in the top-left corner.

Example:

```
// Method signature public static void DrawGUITexture(Rect screenRect,
Texture texture, Material mat = null);
// public static void DrawGUITexture(Rect screenRect, Texture texture,
int leftBorder, int rightBorder, int topBorder, int bottomBorder,
Material mat = null);
public Rect screenRect = new Rect(0, 0, 100, 100);
public Texture theTexture;

private void OnDrawGizmos() {
  if(theTexture != null) {
    Gizmos.DrawGUITexture(screenRect, theTexture);
  }
} Result:
```

DrawFrustrum

The DrawFrustrum draws a camera frustum using the currently set Gizmos.matrix for its location and rotation (don't worry about the meaning of the Gizmos.matrix variable, we will talk about that soon).

Example:

```
// Method signature public static void DrawFrustum(Vector3 center,
float fov, float maxRange, float minRange, float aspect);
public Vector3 center = Vector3.zero;
public float fov = 60;
```

```
public float maxRange = 1;
public float minRange = 3;
public float aspect = 1.3f;

private void OnDrawGizmos() {
  Gizmos.DrawFrustum(
    center, fov, maxRange, minRange, aspect);
}
```

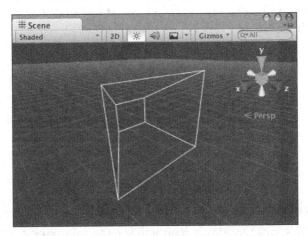

Now, you have all the necessary knowledge to work with gizmos, so apply what you learned to move forward with the development of the Level Creator tool.

Adding a structure to our levels

Open the *Run & Jump* project and look for the folder Scripts/Level. Inside this folder, you will find all the related to the video game. The Level class is responsible for making our levels work.

As you may have noticed, in *Chapter 1*, *Getting Started with Editor Scripting*, all the level piece prefabs are added to the scene and used by the level without a problem, but we don't have control over the size of the level or any way to guarantee that the level piece prefabs are going to be in the right position. Most important, the Level class is not aware about the level piece prefabs present on the level.

We are going to fix this situation making changes to the Level class, adding an array to save references to the level piece prefabs and define it size based in the total columns and rows supported by that array.

Visually, you are going to see the size of the level with the help of a grid made with gizmos.

As this chapter requires changes on the `Level` class, there a couple of things you must know:

- The `Level` class is a partial class, this means that its content is divided in several files: the `Level.cs` and `Level.Logic.cs` scripts. This is just to make its manipulation easier in the book. All the changes will take place in `Level.cs`.

- The Level class follows a **Singleton design** pattern, this means that the instantiation of the class is restricted to just one object and you can have access to this from any other class using the `Level.Instance` method.

- To learn more about Partial classes visit: `https://msdn.microsoft.com/en-us/library/wa80x488(v=vs.140).aspx`
- To learn more about the Singleton design pattern visit the: `https://en.wikipedia.org/wiki/Singleton_pattern`

Implementing the gizmo grid

When you open the script `Level.cs`. You will see the following code:

```
using UnityEngine;

namespace RunAndJump {
  public partial class Level : MonoBehaviour {

    [SerializeField]
    public int _totalTime = 60;
    [SerializeField]
    private float gravity = -30;
    [SerializeField]
    private AudioClip bgm;
    [SerializeField]
    private Sprite background;

    public int TotalTime {
      get { return _totalTime; }
      set { _totalTime = value; }
    }
```

```
public float Gravity {
  get { return gravity; }
  set { gravity = value; }
}

public AudioClip Bgm {
  get { return bgm; }
  set { bgm = value; }
}

public Sprite Background {
  get { return background; }
  set { background = value; }
  }
 }
}
```

This script holds the variables that you saw in the inspector and the properties to access and change these values.

As you may have noticed, making your variables public is not the only way to expose them in the inspector; an alternative is using the SerializeField attribute. We will talk more about this in *Chapter 3, Creating Custom Inspectors*.

Let's make the first change by updating the script to look like this:

```
using UnityEngine;
namespace RunAndJump {
  public partial class Level : MonoBehaviour {

    [SerializeField]
    public int _totalTime = 60;
    [SerializeField]
    private float _gravity = -30;
    [SerializeField]
    private AudioClip _bgm;
    [SerializeField]
    private Sprite _background;
    [SerializeField]
    private int _totalColumns = 25;
    [SerializeField]
    private int _totalRows = 10;
```

```
    public const float GridSize = 1.28f;

    private readonly Color _normalColor = Color.grey;
    private readonly Color _selectedColor = Color.yellow;

    public int TotalTime {
      get { return _totalTime; }
      set { _totalTime = value; }
    }

    public float Gravity {
      get { return _gravity; }
      set { _gravity = value; }
    }

    public AudioClip Bgm {
      get { return _bgm; }
      set { _bgm = value; }
    }

    public Sprite Background {
      get { return _background; }
      set { _background = value; }
    }

    public int TotalColumns {
      get { return _totalColumns; }
      set { _totalColumns = value; }
    }

    public int TotalRows {
      get { return _totalRows; }
      set { _totalRows = value; }
    }
  }
}
```

The variables _totalColumns and _totalRows are going to indicate the total number of level piece prefabs supported in the x and y axis.

The constant GridSize specifies the size of each cell in the grid. The value 1.28f is based on the current size of the level piece prefabs of the video game.

We also added two read-only variables, `_normalColor` and `_selectedColor`, to define the color of the grid depending on its state.

Continuing on `Level.cs`, we will add the following auxiliary methods, `GridFrameGizmo` and `GridGizmo`, to help us in the creation of the gizmo grid:

```
private void GridFrameGizmo(int cols, int rows) {
    Gizmos.DrawLine(new Vector3(0, 0, 0), new Vector3(0, rows *
GridSize, 0));
    Gizmos.DrawLine(new Vector3(0, 0, 0), new Vector3(cols *
GridSize, 0, 0));
    Gizmos.DrawLine(new Vector3(cols * GridSize, 0, 0), new
Vector3(cols * GridSize, rows * GridSize, 0));
    Gizmos.DrawLine(new Vector3(0, rows * GridSize, 0), new
Vector3(cols * GridSize, rows * GridSize, 0));
} private void GridGizmo(int cols, int rows) {
    for (int i = 1 ; i < cols ; i++) {
        Gizmos.DrawLine(new Vector3(i * GridSize, 0, 0), new Vector3(i
* GridSize, rows * GridSize, 0));
    }
    for (int j = 1 ; j < rows ; j++) {
        Gizmos.DrawLine(new Vector3(0, j * GridSize, 0), new
Vector3(cols * GridSize, j * GridSize, 0));
    }
}
```

The method `GridFrameGizmo` creates a rectangle with a width equals to `cols` times `GridSize` and a height equals to rows times `GridSize`.

The `GridGizmo`, using two for loops, creates the vertical and horizontal lines for the grid. To do this, we used the `Gizmos.DrawLine` method.

To see the gizmos working, let's add an `OnDrawGizmos` method and call the methods we created inside it:

```
private void OnDrawGizmos() {
    Color oldColor = Gizmos.color;

    Gizmos.color = _normalColor;
    GridGizmo(_totalColumns, _totalRows);
    GridFrameGizmo(_totalColumns, _totalRows);

    Gizmos.color = oldColor;
}
```

Here, we will use the `Gizmos.color` variable to define the color used to render the gizmos in the **Scene View**. This is a static variable part of the Gizmos class so, as good practice, always save the original color and restore it when you're done using it.

Save the script and wait for Unity to compile it. Then, in the Unity editor menu, navigate to **Tools | Level Creator | New Level Scene** to create a new level, as shown in the following screenshot:

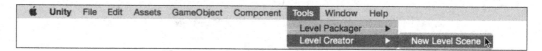

Now, you will see the following in the **Scene View**:

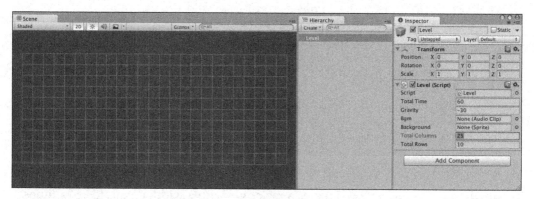

You can adjust the column/row size of the grid by changing the values of **Total Columns** and **Total Rows** in the inspector. The size of the grid is automatically updated.

To add a visual feedback when the `Level` game object is selected, we will use the `OnDrawGizmosSelected` method, changing the color of the grid frame when that happens. Let's add the following:

```
private void OnDrawGizmosSelected() {
  Color oldColor = Gizmos.color;

  Gizmos.color = _selectedColor;
  GridFrameGizmo(_totalColumns, _totalRows);

  Gizmos.color = oldColor;
}
```

As always, wait for the compiler to finish and then select the `Level` game object. You will see the frame on the grid highlighted:

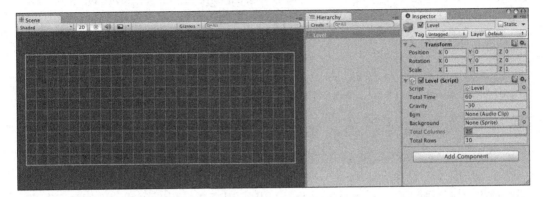

If you select the `Level` game object and change its position, you will notice that the grid remains in the same place. This is because the points passed to the Gizmo's class methods are actually transformed using the Gizmo's matrix before the grid is painted on the **Scene View**, but now the identity matrix is used by default.

For our purposes, this current behavior is okay, but if you want to make the gizmo transform with the game object, the only thing you need to do is change the value of the `Gizmos.matrix` variable. This is a static variable part of the Gizmos class, so as good practice, always save the original matrix and restore it when you're done using it.

For example, the update required by the `OnDrawGizmos` method is as follows:

```
private void OnDrawGizmos() {
  Color oldColor = Gizmos.color;
  Matrix4x4 oldMatrix = Gizmos.matrix;
  Gizmos.matrix = transform.localToWorldMatrix;

  Gizmos.color = _normalColor;
  GridGizmo(_totalColumns, _totalRows);
  GridFrameGizmo(_totalColumns, _totalRows);

  Gizmos.color = oldColor;
  Gizmos.matrix = oldMatrix;
}
```

Implementing the snap to grid behaviour

To create our first level in *Chapter 1, Getting Started with Editor Scripting*, we used a hot key to snap the level piece prefabs between them. Here, we will do the same, but instead of using the hot key, the level piece prefabs are going to snap to the grid automatically.

Here, we will assume that the Level game object position and rotation is always (0,0,0) and the scale is (1,1,1). Also, the **2D mode** is selected by default.

Later, we will work on how keep this configuration by default. Based on the grid we created, we need to implement a few things to achieve our goal:

- A way to convert 3D coordinates to grid coordinates and vice versa
- A way to know when these coordinates are outside the boundaries of the grid

Inside the Level class, add the following methods in the Level.cs script:

```
public Vector3 WorldToGridCoordinates(Vector3 point) {
  Vector3 gridPoint = new Vector3(
  (int)((point.x - transform.position.x) / GridSize) ,
  (int)((point.y - transform.position.y) / GridSize), 0.0f);
  return gridPoint;
}


public Vector3 GridToWorldCoordinates(int col, int row) {
  Vector3 worldPoint = new Vector3(
  transform.position.x + (col * GridSize + GridSize / 2.0f),
  transform.position.y + (row * GridSize + GridSize / 2.0f),
        0.0f);
  return worldPoint;
}
public bool IsInsideGridBounds(Vector3 point) {
  float minX = transform.position.x;
  float maxX = minX + _totalColumns * GridSize;
  float minY = transform.position.y;
  float maxY = minY + _totalRows * GridSize;
  return (point.x >= minX && point.x <= maxX && point.y >= minY &&
point.y <= maxY);
}
```

```
public bool IsInsideGridBounds(int col, int row) {
   return (col >= 0 && col < _totalColumns && row >= 0 && row < _
totalRows);
}
```

The WorldToGridCoordinates method receives a Vector3 point and returns a Vector3 where *x* and *y* correspond to the col and row coordinates in the grid (a Vector3 was used in order to avoid the creation of a new struct).

The GridToWorldCoordinates method receives a col and row position of the grid and returns a Vector3 corresponding to the world coordinates (assuming *z* = 0). The IsInsideGridBounds method has two different signatures. One receives a

Vector3 point and returns true if the coordinates col and row are inside the grid. The other one does the same but instead of a vector, receives a grid coordinate (col, row).

We will start using these methods intensively soon, but for now, just to verify these work properly, let's create a script called SnapToGridTest.cs with the following code (you can discard this script at the end of this chapter):

```
using UnityEngine;
using RunAndJump;

[ExecuteInEditMode]
public class SnapToGridTest: MonoBehaviour {

    private void Update () {
        Vector3 gridCoord = Level.Instance.WorldToGridCoordinates
(transform.position);
        transform.position = Level.Instance.
GridToWorldCoordinates((int)gridCoord.x, (int) gridCoord.y);
    }

    private void OnDrawGizmos () {
        Color oldColor = Gizmos.color;
        Gizmos.color = (Level.Instance.IsInsideGridBounds (transform.
position)) ? Color.green : Color.red;
        Gizmos.DrawCube (transform.position, Vector3.one * Level.
GridSize);
        Gizmos.color = oldColor;
    }
}
```

The `SnapToGridTest.cs` file renders a gizmo cube on the **Scene View**; this will change the color based on its position. With a reference to the level script, the `SnapToGridTest` method will be green if its position is contained by the grid, and red if the opposite happens.

In the `Update` function, we adjusted the position of the game object so it remains snapped to the grid cells. We added a special attribute before the class declaration called `ExecuteInEditMode`. This attribute allows the `Update` function to be called, even when the editor is not in play mode.

> By default, script components are only executed in play mode. By adding the attribute `ExecuteInEditMode`, each script component will also have its callback functions executed while the Editor is not in Play mode. Be careful: the expected behavior have differences compared to the same script running in Play mode, for example, the `Update` function is only called when something in the scene is changed. To get more information about this, visit the following link:
>
> `http://docs.unity3d.com/ScriptReference/`
> `ExecuteInEditMode.html`

Wait for Unity to compile the script and then, with the `Level` game object in the scene, add a few game objects with the `SnapToGridTest.cs` script attached inside the `Level` game object.

Start moving the `SnapToGridTest` game objects inside and outside the grid with the mouse, you will notice that the boundary detection works and changes the color of the gizmo cube while always snapping to the grid:

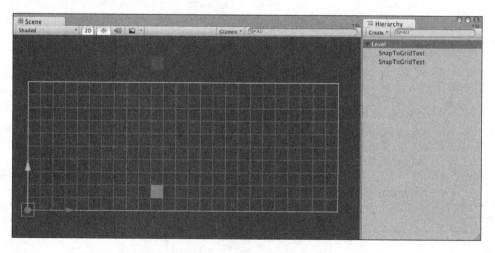

Well done! We've finished our gizmo grid feature.

Summary

In this chapter, you learned about how to use gizmos and continued working with the features of the Level Creator tool by implementing a gizmo grid with an snap to grid feature.

The Gizmos class is part of the `UnityEngine` namespace and allows you to create visual aids in the **Scene View** to work with our scripts.

To render gizmos, we must implement the `OnDrawGizmos` and `OnDrawGizmosSelected` methods in our `MonoBehaviour` classes, and call methods of the Gizmos class to draw the visuals. When it is not possible to access the code of the `MonoBehaviour` class to implement these methods directly, an alternative way is to use the `DrawGizmo` attribute, allowing you to implement the gizmo logic in a second class.

When you work with gizmos, you can change they color and the matrix used to be rendered. To achieve this, you need to overwrite the variables `Gizmos.color` and `Gizmos.matrix`, respectively. Because these variables are static, it's recommended to always save the current value of the variables and restore it when you're done.

Gizmos can help visually expose implementation details of code to artists and designers, and help them debug problems on the fly. Think about gizmos as a way to expose part of the code to team members who are not programmers. If an image is worth a thousand words, a good gizmo is worth more than a thousand lines of debugging code.

In the next chapter, we will continue working with the Level Creator tool by creating our own custom inspectors.

3
Creating Custom Inspectors

When you've worked on a Unity project for a long time, you know that the bigger your scripts get, the more unwieldy they become; all your public variables take up space in the **Inspector** window, and as they accumulate, they begin to convert into one giant and scary monster.

Sometimes, organization is the trick, like separating these variables in logic groups in your MonoBehaviour class, but the approach is not always enough to make inspectors user friendly.

To solve this problem, Unity allows us to create **custom inspectors** for our scripts, so we can define how our exposed variables and their properties should look in the **Inspector** window.

Here, you will learn how to have a custom inspector up and running by creating one for the Level class in *Run & Jump*.

In this chapter, we will cover the following topics:

- The CustomEditor attribute
- Inspector messages
- Creating a GUI
- Using layouts
- Property Drawers and Decorator Drawers
- The SerializedObject and SerializedProperty classes

Overview

The **Inspector** window displays detailed information about all the attached components and scripts of the currently selected game object. The following is an example of how the **Inspector** window looks. In this case, we are using the **HazzardSpikes** level piece prefab from *Run & Jump*.

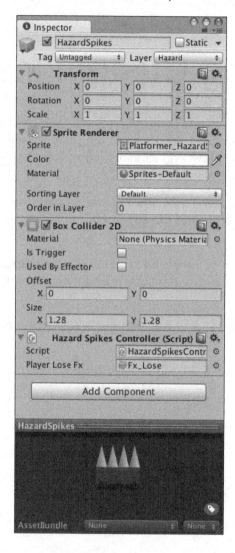

You can use the inspectors to change properties and exposed variables from a component or script; at runtime, you can use them to find the right combination of values for your video game.

In a script, if you define a public variable of an object type (such as `GameObject` or `Transform`), you can drag and drop a game object or prefab into the inspector to make the assignment.

In this chapter, you will learn how to create custom inspector by following our own specifications and not the Unity default ones. In this case, we will work over the `Level` class inspector to make it part of the Level Creator tool workflow.

Defining the chapter goals

In this chapter, we will improve the `Level` class and use it to save the references of the level piece prefabs used on a level. Here, we will try to have control over the level size constraints. In this process, we will improve how we deal with these constraints and other variables of the level by creating a custom inspector.

The goals here are:

- Saving references of all the level piece prefabs on the level in the `Level` class
- Creating a custom inspector to expose the variables of the Level class, taking care to have a user-friendly way to resize the level in terms of columns and rows
- Improving the general look of the custom inspector by changing the way the properties are displayed using complex layouts
- Improving how certain properties are displayed using property drawers

The final result will look like this:

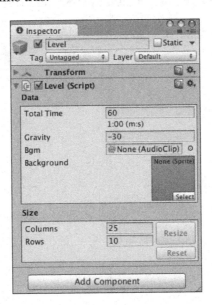

Upgrading the Level class

In this video game, a level is just a Unity scene with several level piece prefabs aligned with each other. When we started this project, we took a look at how the level scenes were implemented and found that there was no relation between these prefabs and the Level class through code.

In the last chapter, we added gizmos to display a grid and the necessary methods to make game objects snap to this grid. Now, the focus is to make the Level class capable of knowing what is on the level scene.

To the Level class, we will add an array to handle a 2D matrix of LevelPieces, the base class of the level piece prefabs in *Run & Jump*. Its size will be determined explicitly by two variables, that is, the total number of columns and rows in the grid.

Go to the Scripts/Level folder and open the Level.cs script. Add the following code to the class:

```
[SerializeField]
private LevelPiece[] _pieces;

public LevelPiece[] Pieces {
get { return _pieces; }
    set { _pieces = value; }
}
```

Save the script and wait for Unity to compile it. Then, in the Unity editor menu, navigate to **Tools | Level Creator | New Level Scene** to create a new level:

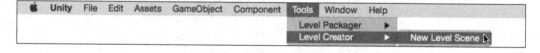

Select the level game object. If everything is OK, you will see something like this:

Now we are ready to go!

Understanding how an inspector works

Every time you attach a MonoBehaviour script to a game object, all the public variables in that script are automatically exposed in the inspector. This means you can change the values directly from there and also these values are serialized.

 Serialization is the process of converting an object into a stream of bytes in order to store the object or transmit it to memory, a database, or a file. Its main purpose is to save the state of an object to be able to recreate it when needed.

Making your variables public is not the only way to expose them in the Inspector. An alternative is using the SerializeField attribute, like in the Level class variables, so independent of the access modifier of the property (public, private, protected, or internal), this will be exposed and serialized without exception.

In specific scenarios, you might want to have a public property to be serialized without exposing it in the inspector. For this, you must use the HideInInspector attribute.

In the following example, you will see a script using the SerializeField attribute and HideInInspector attribute, part of the UnityEngine namespace, and the respective inspector rendered, as follows:

```
using UnityEngine;

public class InspectorExample : MonoBehaviour {
    public int variableA = 100;
    [SerializeField]
    private int variableB = 200;
    // This variable won't be exposed in the inspector
    [HideInInspector]
    public int variableC = 300;
}
```

You will see the following output:

There is a direct relationship with the types Unity is able to serialize and the ones exposed in the inspector. The supported types are as follows:

- All classes inheriting from UnityEngine.Object, for example GameObject, Component, MonoBehaviour, Texture2D, and AnimationClip

- All basic data types, such as `int`, `string`, `float`, and `bool`
- Some built-in types, such as `Vector2`, `Vector3`, `Vector4`, `Quaternion`, `Matrix4x4`, `Color`, `Rect`, and `LayerMaski`
- Arrays of a serializable type
- List of a serializable type
- Enums
- Structs

Now, talking about the inspector, if the default behavior is not enough to satisfy the necessities of your project, because the resulting interface is not user friendly, you need a special kind of validation/interaction or if your data structure wasn't in the previous list, you will need to create your custom one.

Creating a custom inspector

In this section, we will create the base structure to start using custom inspectors in our project.

Using the CustomEditor attribute

The `CustomEditor` attribute is part of the `UnityEditor` namespace and is the way Unity binds an editor script with a specific type of the `MonoBehaviour` class to modify the way the default inspector works.

 To use the `CustomEditor` attribute, you must place your script inside an `Editor` folder, or in a folder nested inside an `Editor` folder.

Create a script called `LevelInspector.cs` inside the folder `Tools\LevelCreator\Editor`, and then add the following code:

```
using UnityEngine;
using UnityEditor;

namespace RunAndJump.LevelCreator {
    [CustomEditor(typeof(Level))]
    public class LevelInspector : Editor {

    }
}
```

The attribute CustomEditor expects a type. In this case, we passed the type Level. Doing this, you will overwrite the inspector of all the Level class instances in Unity.

Your must extend from the Editor class and in this way you will have access to all the methods and properties to create custom inspectors.

> When you create a custom inspector for a type of class, if you try to select several instances in the editor to make changes at the same time, Unity will not allow you to do so. To support multi-object editing, you must use the CanEditMultipleObjects attribute. Add this before the class declaration. In this case, we will have just one Level class instance at a time, so this is not necessary.

Save and wait for Unity to compile the script. Once it finishes, you will not see any visual difference.

Don't worry, breathe deeply and relax; this was expected. We did the base setup but we aren't doing anything to overwrite the normal behavior of the inspector. In the next section, we will explore the methods to get a working custom inspector.

Playing with the inspector message methods and target variable

Like the Awake, Update, and OnDestroy methods in the MonoBehaviour classes, known as the message methods, inspectors have their own ones to handle similar kind of actions inherited from the Editor class.

Let's implement these in our LevelInspector class:

```
using UnityEngine;
using UnityEditor;

namespace RunAndJump.LevelCreator {
    [CustomEditor(typeof(Level))]
    public class LevelInspector : Editor {

        private Level _myTarget;

        private void OnEnable () {
            Debug.Log ("OnEnable was called...");
            _myTarget = (Level)target;
        }
```

```
        private void OnDisable () {
            Debug.Log ("OnDisable was called...");
        }

        private void OnDestroy () {
            Debug.Log ("OnDestroy was called...");
        }

        public override void OnInspectorGUI () {
            EditorGUILayout.LabelField ("The GUI of this inspector was
modified.");
            EditorGUILayout.LabelField ("The current level time is: "
+ _myTarget.TotalTime);
        }
    }
}
```

The OnEnable method is called every time the inspected object is selected. This is a good place for all the initialization code.

The OnDisable method is called when the inspected object goes out of scope. This is also called when the object is destroyed and can be used for any cleanup code.

The OnDestroy method is called when the inspected object will be destroyed.

> When scripts are reloaded after the compilation has finished, OnDisable is called, followed by OnEnable after the script has been loaded.

The Editor class has a variable called target. This variable has a reference to the object inspected and it is used to access the properties of that object and to manipulate them in the custom inspector.

> If your script supports multi-object editing, you must use targets instead of target. This will return a Unity object array with all the objects being inspected.

Because target returns a Unity object, we must cast this to a Level type to access the public methods and variables of the inspected object. We will save this reference in the variable _myTarget and do the initialization inside the OnEnable method.

The last method we need to implement is OnInspectorGUI. In this method, you can add methods to render the inspector GUI. This one must to be overridden in order to work and you need to keep the access modifier as public.

As an example, we added two labels to the inspector, and in the second one, we used the _myTarget variable to access the TotalTime property of the inspected Level class.

This is how our inspector looks now:

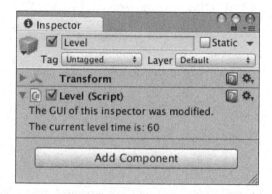

Good work! In the next section, we will continue working in the GUI for this custom inspector.

 If you want to check more about the Editor class, visit:
http://docs.unity3d.com/ScriptReference/Editor.html.

Adding the GUI elements

Before we start working in the new GUI, let's see how to make this custom inspector render the default GUI. Let's update the OnInspectorGUI method:

```
public override void OnInspectorGUI () {
    DrawDefaultInspector ();
}
```

Save and wait for Unity to compile the script. The DrawDefaultInspector method will display the default GUI on the inspector.

 You can use this method to help you debug your custom inspector for troubleshooting.

We want to split the task of creating this custom inspector in two parts:

- **Data**: This part exposes the total time, gravity, BGM, and background variables.

- **The Resize feature**: This part has the necessary GUI to allow a game designer to resize the level.

Let's start with the first part. In the LevelInspector class, we will modify the OnInspectorGUI method again and use a new method created by us called DrawLevelDataGUI:

```
public override void OnInspectorGUI () {
  // DrawDefaultInspector();
  DrawLevelDataGUI ();
}

private void DrawLevelDataGUI () {
  EditorGUILayout.LabelField ("Data", EditorStyles.boldLabel);
  _myTarget.TotalTime = EditorGUILayout.IntField ("Total Time", Mathf.
  Max (0, _myTarget.TotalTime));
  _myTarget.Gravity = EditorGUILayout.FloatField ("Gravity",
  _myTarget.Gravity);
  _myTarget.Bgm = (AudioClip)EditorGUILayout.ObjectField ("Bgm",
  _myTarget.Bgm, typeof(AudioClip), false);
  _myTarget.Background = (Sprite)EditorGUILayout.ObjectField
  ("Background", _myTarget.Background, typeof(Sprite), false);
}
```

The EditorGUILayout class has several methods to draw an editor GUI. All the methods in this class adapt automatically to the inspector following layout restrictions. You will find similar methods in the EditorGUI class, but the difference is that, on this class, you must specify the rectangle that will contain the GUI element for each one of its methods.

The EditorGUILayout and EditorGUI classes are too big to be covered thoroughly in this book, so check the following URLs to get an idea about the options these classes gives us:

- http://docs.unity3d.com/ScriptReference/
  EditorGUILayout.html
- http://docs.unity3d.com/ScriptReference/
  EditorGUI.html

We used the `EditorGUILayout` class to create several fields. Let's review these:

`LabelField` was used to display a label with the text data. As a second parameter, we passed a variable from the class `EditorStyles` to change the style of the font used by the label - bold style (in *Chapter 6, Changing the Look and Feel of the Editor with GUI Styles and GUI Skins* we will talk more about how to change the look and feel of our tools).

The `IntField` and `FloatField` methods work in the same way: both show an editable text field that allows only integers and floats.

The first parameter is the label for the field and the second one is a reference to the variable used to extract the value displayed in the field. The methods return an integer and a float, respectively; so, you can use these values to overwrite the variables inspected.

`ObjectField` method is used for objects and requires the type of the object and a Boolean used as a flag to specify whether objects on the scene can be added to this field or not. In our case, we don't require that. The returning value must to be casted.

Save the changes and go back to Unity. Create a new level scene and you should see the following:

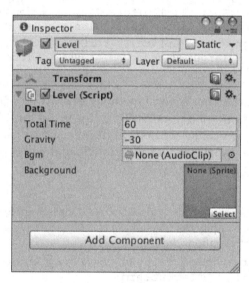

If you try to change the **Total Time** field to a negative value, the inspector is not going to allow you because we used the method `Max` from the class `Mathf` to always guarantee that `TotalTime` will be equal to or greater than 0. This means, with a custom inspector, we can improve the validation of all the parameters our game object or component is going to use.

Implementing the resize feature

To start, add the following two variables to the `LevelInspector` class:

```
private int _newTotalColumns;
private int _newTotalRows;
```

These variables are going to be used to save the new Level size values to previsualize the changes. As soon we decide to proceed with the change, we will update the values `TotalColumns` and `TotalRows` and do the changes to the `Pieces` array.

The `LevelInspector` class will be responsible for the initialization of the `Pieces` array because we want to make this happen in an editor context.

In the `LevelInspector` class, create two methods called `InitLevel` and `ResetResizeValues`. These are going to be called inside the `OnEnable` method:

```
private void OnEnable () {
    // Debug.Log ("OnEnable was called...");
    _myTarget = (Level)target;
    InitLevel ();
    ResetResizeValues ();
}

private void InitLevel () {
    if (_myTarget.Pieces == null || _myTarget.Pieces.Length == 0) {
        Debug.Log("Initializing the Pieces array...");
        _myTarget.Pieces = new LevelPiece[ _myTarget.TotalColumns *
_myTarget.TotalRows];
    }
}

private void ResetResizeValues () {
    _newTotalColumns = _myTarget.TotalColumns;
    _newTotalRows = _myTarget.TotalRows;
}
```

Now, to do the resize, we need to change the length of the `Pieces` array and remove all the `LevelPiece` instances out of level bounds, destroying the prefab associated to the instances. We will add this in the `LevelInspector` class using the name `ResizeLevel`:

```
private void ResizeLevel () {
    LevelPiece [] newPieces = new LevelPiece [_newTotalColumns * _
newTotalRows];
    for (int col = 0; col < _myTarget.TotalColumns; ++col) {
        for (int row = 0; row < _myTarget.TotalRows; ++row) {
            if (col < _newTotalColumns && row < _newTotalRows) {
                newPieces [col + row * _newTotalColumns] =
                    _myTarget.Pieces [col + row * _myTarget.
TotalColumns];
            } else {
                LevelPiece piece = _myTarget.Pieces [col + row * _
myTarget.TotalColumns];
                if (piece != null) {
                    // we must to use DestroyImmediate in a Editor
context
                    Object.DestroyImmediate (piece.gameobject);
                }
            }
        }
    }
    _myTarget.Pieces = newPieces;
    _myTarget.TotalColumns = _newTotalColumns;
    _myTarget.TotalRows = _newTotalRows;
}
```

With the logic done, in the next section, we will implement the GUI we are missing, which is necessary to make the resize.

Using buttons to trigger actions

In the `LevelInspector` class, we will modify the `OnInspectorGUI` method, adding a new method created by us, called `DrawLevelSizeGUI`:

```
public override void OnInspectorGUI () {
    // DrawDefaultInspector();
    DrawLevelDataGUI ();
    DrawLevelSizeGUI ();
}
private void DrawLevelSizeGUI () {
    EditorGUILayout.LabelField ("Size", EditorStyles.boldLabel);
```

```
   _newTotalColumns = EditorGUILayout.IntField ("Columns", Mathf.Max
(1, _newTotalColumns));
   _newTotalRows = EditorGUILayout.IntField ("Rows", Mathf.Max (1, _
newTotalRows));
   // with this variable we can enable or disable GUI
   bool oldEnabled = GUI.enabled;
   GUI.enabled = (_newTotalColumns != _myTarget.TotalColumns || _
newTotalRows != _myTarget.TotalRows);
   bool buttonResize = GUILayout.Button ("Resize", GUILayout.Height (2
* EditorGUIUtility.singleLineHeight));
   if (buttonResize) {
     if (EditorUtility.DisplayDialog (
       "Level Creator",
       "Are you sure you want to resize the level?\nThis action cannot
be undone.",
       "Yes",
       "No")) {
       ResizeLevel ();
     }
   }
   bool buttonReset = GUILayout.Button ("Reset");
   if (buttonReset) {
       ResetResizeValues ();
   }
   GUI.enabled = oldEnabled;
 }
```

The beginning of the code is pretty similar to the DrawLevelDataGUI method; the only difference is the usage of the method Button from the class GUILayout.

Button is a method that renders a Button. To check whether the user is clicking on the button, we need to evaluate this method, returning true when clicked, false in other cases.

Here, two buttons were created, the first one with the name Resize, which will display a popup dialog if clicked on, thanks to the method DisplayDialog from the class EditorUtility. If the level designer clicks on Yes, the method ResizeLevel will be called.

The second button called Reset restores the variables _newTotalColumns and _newTotalRows to match the TotalColumns and TotalRows values, respectively.

As it makes no sense to press the Resize or Reset buttons if the values for the columns or the rows don't differ, we will disable the buttons using the variable enabled from the class GUI.

If GUI.enabled is false, all the interactive GUI components, such as buttons, will be disabled; the opposite happens when it is true. Remember to always save the original value and then restore it when you are done.

> As you may have noticed, you have more classes to get GUI stuff related than EditorGUI and EditorGUILayout; you will be able to use GUI and GUILayout too. To learn more about these two classes, visit the following two websites:
>
> * http://docs.unity3d.com/ScriptReference/GUI.html
> * http://docs.unity3d.com/ScriptReference/GUILayout.html

At this point, the aspect of the inspector will be as follows:

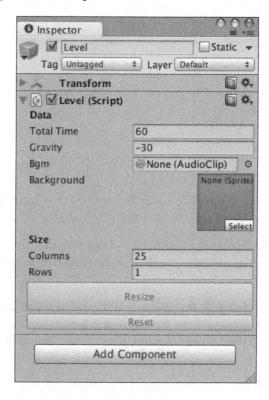

The buttons are disabled by default until you change the values of the **Column** or **Row** fields:

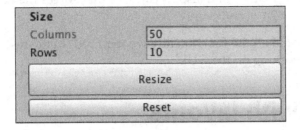

If you click on **Resize**, the following popup will appear:

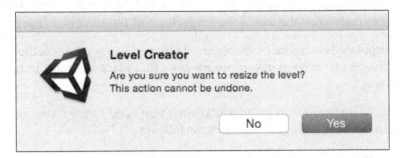

If you click on **Yes**, the array of pieces will be updated, but unless you move the mouse cursor over the Scene View, you will still see the level grid without any size change.

This happens because, when you pass the mouse over the Scene View, you force the redrawing of the visible elements. We need to force this in order to make the resize functionality look correct.

To do this, we will use the flag changed for the class GUI. This will be true if there is any change to the Inspector GUI. Let's update the OnInspectorGUI function again:

```
public override void OnInspectorGUI () {
    // DrawDefaultInspector ();
    DrawLevelDataGUI ();
    DrawLevelSizeGUI ();

    if(GUI.changed) {
        EditorUtility.SetDirty(_myTarget);
    }
}
```

The `SetDirty` object, part of the `EditorUtility` class, marks the target object as dirty. Unity internally uses the dirty flag to find out when assets have changed and need to be saved to disk; and also, because of this, forces the `Level` class to be redrawn.

We have implemented all the functionality we required. In the rest of this chapter, we will continue working on the GUI.

Working with layouts

We have explained the `EditorGUILayout` and `GUILayout` class, which have several GUI elements that adapt automatically to the inspector following the layout restrictions. By default, all these elements stack in a vertical way, so the first element you call in your code is on the top of the inspector and the last one at the bottom.

You can manipulate how these elements are displayed using a few methods from the `EditorGUILayout` class. We will explore the ones that place elements in horizontal and vertical ways.

To place your GUI elements in a horizontal way, you need to use a couple of methods from the `EditorGUILayout` class, as follows:

```
EditorGUILayout.BeginHorizontal();
// GUI element 1
// GUI element 2
// GUI element 3
EditorGUILayout.EndHorizontal();
```

You will get something like this:

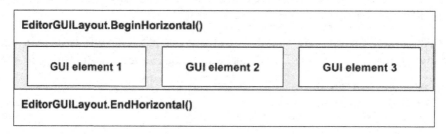

To place your GUI elements in a vertical way, you need to use a couple of methods from the `EditorGUILayout` class, as follows:

```
EditorGUILayout.BeginVertical();
// GUI element 1
// GUI element 2
```

```
// GUI element 3
EditorGUILayout.EndVertical();
```

You will get something like this:

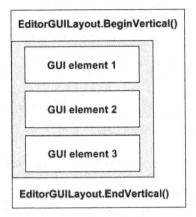

You can always nest different layout arrangements to create more complex layouts. To demonstrate this, we will improve how the GUI from `DrawLevelSizeGUI` is displayed.

Creating complex layouts

Using the current code from the `DrawLevelSizeGUI` method, we will change how the different GUI elements are placed using layouts. To have a better idea about how to mix the horizontal and vertical layouts, let's look at the following diagram:

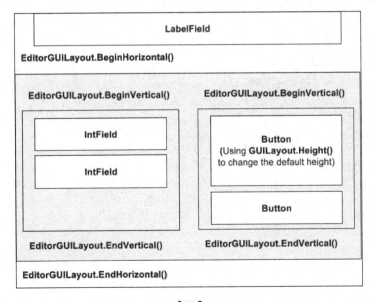

Based on this diagram, we will place the layout methods as follows:

```
private void DrawLevelSizeGUI () {
  EditorGUILayout.LabelField ("Size", EditorStyles.boldLabel);
  EditorGUILayout.BeginHorizontal ("box");
  EditorGUILayout.BeginVertical ();
  _newTotalColumns = EditorGUILayout.IntField ("Columns", Mathf.Max
(1, _newTotalColumns));
  _newTotalRows = EditorGUILayout.IntField ("Rows", Mathf.Max (1, _
newTotalRows));

  EditorGUILayout.EndVertical ();
  EditorGUILayout.BeginVertical ();

  // with this variable we can enable or disable GUI
  bool oldEnabled = GUI.enabled;
  GUI.enabled = (_newTotalColumns != _myTarget.TotalColumns || _
newTotalRows != _myTarget.TotalRows);
  bool buttonResize = GUILayout.Button ("Resize", GUILayout.Height (2
* EditorGUIUtility.singleLineHeight));
  if (buttonResize) {
    if (EditorUtility.DisplayDialog (
      "Level Creator",
      "Are you sure you want to resize the level?\nThis action cannot
be undone.",
      "Yes",
      "No")) {
      ResizeLevel ();
    }
  }
  bool buttonReset = GUILayout.Button ("Reset");
  if (buttonReset) {
    ResetResizeValues ();
  }
  GUI.enabled = oldEnabled;

  EditorGUILayout.EndVertical ();
  EditorGUILayout.EndHorizontal ();
}
```

If you check the level custom inspector, you will see something like this:

To the first `EditorGUILayout.BeginHorizontal` method, we passed a parameter, which is a string with the value box; this is a way to use GUIStyles in our components. Again, this will be covered soon in *Chapter 6, Changing the Look and Feel of the Editor with GUI Styles and GUI Skins*, but for now, gives a nice touch to our inspector.

Let's do the same to the top part of the inspector by updating the method `DrawLevelDataGUI`:

```
private void DrawLevelDataGUI () {
    EditorGUILayout.LabelField ("Data", EditorStyles.boldLabel);
    EditorGUILayout.BeginVertical ("box");
    _myTarget.TotalTime = EditorGUILayout.IntField ("Total Time",
Mathf.Max (0, _myTarget.TotalTime));
    _myTarget.Gravity = EditorGUILayout.FloatField ("Gravity", _
myTarget.Gravity);
    _myTarget.Bgm = (AudioClip)EditorGUILayout.ObjectField ("Bgm",
_myTarget.Bgm, typeof(AudioClip), false);
    _myTarget.Background = (Sprite)EditorGUILayout.ObjectField
("Background", _myTarget.Background, typeof(Sprite), false);
    EditorGUILayout.EndVertical ();
}
```

At this point, your inspector should look like this:

We are getting closer to the final result, but before we continue, let's look at another way to add custom GUIs to our inspectors.

Improving the inspector without custom inspectors

In this section, we will explore a way to create custom GUI for our properties using Property Drawers.

What is a Property Drawer?

A **Property Drawer** allows you to control how the GUI of a `Serializable` class or property is displayed in the **Inspector** window. This approach significantly reduces the amount of work you have to do for the GUI customization because you don't need to write an entire custom inspector. Instead, you can just apply appropriate attributes to variables in your scripts to tell the editor how you want those properties to be drawn.

Unity has several built-in Property Drawers. In the following example, we will use the `Range` attribute:

```
using UnityEngine;

public class DrawerExample : MonoBehaviour {
   [Range (0, 100)]
   public int intValue = 50;
}
```

This is the result of the preceding code:

Using the `Range` attribute, we rendered a slider that moves between 0 and 100 instead of the common int field without creating a custom inspector.

In the next section, we will check the rest of the available Property Drawers in Unity.

Built-in Property Drawers

The Unity documentation has information about the built-in Property Drawers, but there is no place where you can check all the available ones listed. In this section, we want to resolve this.

Range

The range attribute is used to constrain a float or int variable in a script to a specific range. When this attribute is used, the float or int will be shown as a slider in the inspector instead of the default int or float field:

```
// Method signatures
// public RangeAttribute(float min, float max);
// public RangeAttribute(int min, int max);
[Range (0, 1)]
public float floatRange = 0.5f;
[Range (0, 100)]
public int intRange = 50;
```

You will get the following output:

Multiline

The multiline attribute is used to make a string value to be shown in a Multiline text area. You can set up how many lines of text to make room for. The default is three and the text doesn't wrap on this GUI component:

```
// Method signatures
// public MultilineAttribute();
// public MultilineAttribute(int lines);
[Multiline (2)]
public string stringMultiline = "This text is using a multiline
property drawer";
```

You will get the following output:

TextArea

The `TextArea` attribute makes a string editable within a height-flexible and scrollable text area. You can specify the minimum and maximum values and a scrollbar will appear if the text is bigger than the area available:

```
// Method signatures
// public TextAreaAttribute();
// public TextAreaAttribute(int minLines, int maxLines);
[TextArea (2, 4)]
public string stringTextArea = "This text \nis using \na text area \
nproperty \ndrawer";
```

You will get the following output:

ContextMenu

This Attribute makes a method accessible in the context menu of a component or script. When the user selects this context menu item, the method will be executed. In this example, we will expose the method `DoSomething`:

```
// Method signature
// public ContextMenuAttribute(string name);
    [ContextMenu ("Do Something")]
  public void DoSomething() {
    Debug.Log ("DoSomething was called...");
  }
```

You will get the following output:

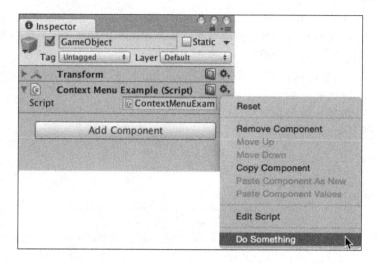

ContextMenuItem

This Attribute makes a method accessible as a context menu item of a property (the method must be nonstatic). In this example, we call a method to reset the value of the `IntReset` variable to 0:

```
// Method signature
// public ContextMenuItemAttribute(string name, string function);
[ContextMenuItem("Reset this value", "Reset")]
public int intReset = 100;

public void Reset() {
    intReset = 0;
}
```

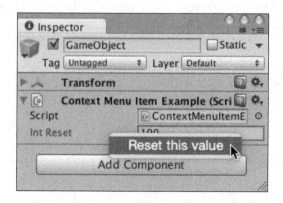

Built-in Decorator Drawers

There are another kind of drawers called **Decorator Drawers**. They are similar in composition to the Property Drawers, but the main difference is that Decorator Drawers are designed to draw decoration in the inspector and are unassociated with a specific field.

While you can only declare one property drawer per variable, you can stack multiple decorator drawers.

Header

This is the attribute that adds a header to some fields in the inspector:

```
// Method signature
// public HeaderAttribute(string header);
[Header("This is a group of variables")]
public int varA = 10;
public int varB = 20;
```

Space

This attribute adds some spacing in the inspector:

```
// Method signature
// public SpaceAttribute(float height);
public int varC = 10;
[Space(40)]
public int varD = 20;
```

Tooltip

The attribute adds a tooltip to a property on the inspector:

```
// Method signature
// public TooltipAttribute(string tooltip);
[Tooltip("This is a tooltip")]
public int varE = 30;
```

Creating you own Property Drawers

If you have a serializable parameter or structure that repeats constantly in your video game and you would like to improve how this renders in the inspector, you can try to write your own property drawers.

We are going to create a property drawer for an integer meant to be a variable to save time in seconds. This Property Drawer will draw a normal int field but also a label with the number of seconds converted to the *m:s* or *h:m:s* time format.

This is going to convert something like this:

To this following output:

For sure, this is much easier to read compared to the previous version.

To implement a Property Drawer you must create two scripts:

- The attribute, the one you will be using over the properties in your MonoBehaviour scripts.

- The drawer, responsible for rendering the GUI and handling the input of the user. This last one is an editor script.

Let's start with the first one. Inside the folder Tools\LevelCreator\Scripts, create a script called TimeAttribute.cs with the following code:

```
using UnityEngine;

namespace RunAndJump.LevelCreator {
  public class TimeAttribute : PropertyAttribute {
    public readonly bool DisplayHours;

    public TimeAttribute (bool displayHours = false) {
      DisplayHours = displayHours;
    }
  }
}
```

Here, we defined the name of the attribute and its parameters. You must create your attribute class extending from the PropertyAttribute class, and if you want to start creating your own, you must have these kind of scripts outside any Editor folder. This is very important to make them work!

 By convention, the name of the attribute class ends with the word attribute. While not required, this is recommended for readability. When the attribute is used, the word attribute is optional.

The TimeAttribute has an optional parameter called DisplayHours. By default, the Time attribute will display a label under the int field with the time in *m:s* format; if DisplayHours is true, this will be displayed in the *h:m:s* format.

Now, we want to implement the drawer. This script must be in an Editor folder. So, inside Tools\LevelCreator\Editor, create a new script called TimeDrawer.cs with the following code:

```
using UnityEngine;
using UnityEditor;
```

```
namespace RunAndJump.LevelCreator {
  [CustomPropertyDrawer (typeof(TimeAttribute))]
  public class TimeDrawer : PropertyDrawer {
    public override float GetPropertyHeight (SerializedProperty
property, GUIContent label) {
      return EditorGUI.GetPropertyHeight (property) * 2;
    }

    public override void OnGUI (Rect position, SerializedProperty
property, GUIContent label) {
      if (property.propertyType == SerializedPropertyType.Integer) {
        property.intValue = EditorGUI.IntField (new Rect (position.x,
position.y, position.width, position.height / 2), label, Mathf.Max (0,
property.intValue));
        EditorGUI.LabelField (new Rect (position.x, position.y +
position.height / 2, position.width, position.height / 2), " ",
TimeFormat (property.intValue));

      } else {
        EditorGUI.HelpBox (position, "To use the Time attribute \"" +
label.text + "\" must be an int!", MessageType.Error);
      }
    }

    private string TimeFormat (int totalSeconds) {
      TimeAttribute time = attribute as TimeAttribute;
      // Here we are using string.Format to add the variables in the
string.
      if (time.DisplayHours) {
        int hours = totalSeconds / (60 * 60);
        int minutes = ((totalSeconds % (60 * 60)) / 60);
        int seconds = (totalSeconds % 60);
        return string.Format ("{0}:{1}:{2} (h:m:s)", hours, minutes.
ToString ().PadLeft (2, '0'), seconds.ToString ().PadLeft (2, '0'));
      } else {
        int minutes = (totalSeconds / 60);
        int seconds = (totalSeconds % 60);
        return string.Format ("{0}:{1} (m:s)", minutes.ToString (),
seconds.ToString ().PadLeft (2, '0'));
      }
    }
  }
}
```

A property drawer doesn't support layouts to create a GUI. For this reason, the only classes usable here are `EditorGUI` and `GUI` (instead of `EditorGUILayout` and `GUILayout`). This class requires a little extra effort to be used; you must define a `Rect` that will contain the GUI element each time you want to use one.

The `CustomPropertyDrawer` attribute is part of the `UnityEditor` namespace and is the way Unity has to bind a drawer with a `Property` attribute. In this case, we passed the type `TimeAttribute`.

You must extend from the `PropertyDrawer` class, and in this way, you will have access to the core methods to create property drawers:

- `GetPropertyHeight`: The responsibility of this method is to handle the height of the drawer. You need to overwrite this method in order to use it.

- `OnGUI`: This is where you place all the code related to render the GUI in a similar way that we did for the inspectors. The only difference here is that you must use the class `EditorGUI` because layouts are not allowed.

You can create Decorator Drawers too by following the steps we did to create a Property Drawer, but instead of extending your drawer from `PropertyDrawer`, you will need to extend it from `DecoratorDrawer`.

To test our code, create a new script called `TimeDrawerDemo.cs` and add the following (you can discard this script later):

```
using UnityEngine;
using RunAndJump.LevelCreator;

public class TimeExample : MonoBehaviour {

    [Time]
    public int TimeMinutes = 3600;
    [Time(true)]
    public int TimeHours = 3600;
    [Time]
    public float TimeError = 3600;
}
```

We added the line using the `RunAndJump.LevelCreator` namespace because the time attribute is part of that namespace. After compiling, if you attach this script to a game object, you will see something like this on the inspector:

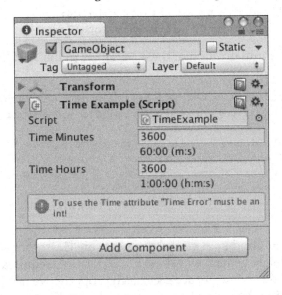

Now with our own custom property drawer working, you will learn how to combine this with the custom inspector we created.

Using drawers inside a custom inspector

We use the variable `target` to access the public methods, properties, and variables of the `Level` class. This is not the only way to do this, and in fact, the alternative way will give us more information related to the properties of the object inspected.

To do this, we will use the classes `SerializedObject` and `SerializedProperty`.

Using SerializedObject and SerializedProperty

Let's declare a few variables in the `LevelInspector` class:

```
private SerializedObject _mySerializedObject;
private SerializedProperty _serializedTotalTime;
```

Now, let's declare the initialization of these variables in the `InitLevel` method:

```
private void InitLevel () {
  _mySerializedObject = new SerializedObject (_myTarget);
  _serializedTotalTime = _mySerializedObject.FindProperty ("_
totalTime");
  if (_myTarget.Pieces == null || _myTarget.Pieces.Length == 0) {
    Debug.Log("Initializing the Pieces array...");
    _myTarget.Pieces = new LevelPiece[ _myTarget.TotalColumns * _
myTarget.TotalRows];
  }
}
```

The `SerializedObject` and `SerializedProperty` are classes for editing properties of objects in a completely generic way. `SerializedObject` requires a reference of the variable target to work; and, to get access to each property, we need to write the name in an explicit way using the `FindProperty` method from the `SerializedObject` class.

It's true that this approach requires extra effort to access each property, but in this way, we get a few benefits, such as handling the undo of the properties by default and accessing information about the property that can be used, for example, to render the property using `PropertyAttibutes`.

To see this last thing in action, in the `Level` class, add the `Time` attribute to the variable `TotalTime`, as follows:

```
[LevelCreator.Time]
public int TotalTime = 60;
```

Then, we will update the `DrawLevelDataGUI` method from the same class by replacing the `IntField` for the `PropertyField` method from the `EditorGUILayout` class. This method takes a `SerializedProperty` reference to render the default GUI from that kind of property.

```
private void DrawLevelDataGUI () {
    EditorGUILayout.LabelField ("Data", EditorStyles.boldLabel);
    EditorGUILayout.BeginVertical ("box");
    //_myTarget.TotalTime = EditorGUILayout.IntField ("Total Time",
Mathf.Max (0, _myTarget.TotalTime));
    EditorGUILayout.PropertyField (_serializedTotalTime);
    _myTarget.Gravity = EditorGUILayout.FloatField ("Gravity", _
myTarget.Gravity);
    _myTarget.Bgm = (AudioClip)EditorGUILayout.ObjectField ("Bgm", _
myTarget.Bgm, typeof(AudioClip), false);
    _myTarget.Background = (Sprite)EditorGUILayout.ObjectField
("Background", _myTarget.Background, typeof(Sprite), false);
    EditorGUILayout.EndVertical ();
}
```

Save the changes. Now, the `Level` class has a custom inspector and one of its properties is using a property drawer to render the GUI. With this, we are done for this chapter:

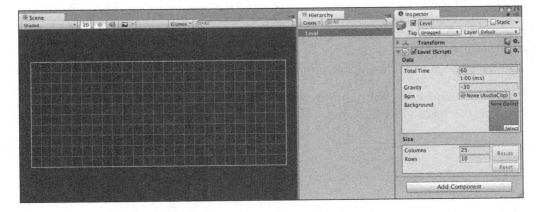

Summary

In this chapter, we learned how to create custom inspectors.

The `CustomEditor` class is part of the `UnityEditor` namespace and it's necessary to make a class a custom inspector. This class must inherit from the `Editor` class and must be nested in an `Editor` folder in order to work.

An inspector, such as a `MonoBehaviour` class, has its own message method. These events are `OnEnable`, `OnDisable`, and `OnDestroy`. To make changes to the GUI, you must override the method `OnInspectorGUI`.

There are several classes to add the GUI in the inspector: the `EditorGUILayout` and `EditorGUI` classes are similar, with the only difference being that the first one auto adapts the GUI elements based in a layout, and the second one requires the specification of a rectangle to be used as a container of the element.

There is a class called `GUILayout`, with generic GUI elements that can be used in a video game or editor context. The `Button` method is part of this class.

It's important to review the API reference of these classes because there are several useful methods to create GUI elements and knowing them makes it easy to make design decisions. Also, exploring the different signatures that each method on the API has will help you to customize how these GUI elements are rendered.

Without having to write a custom inspector, it is possible to create a GUI for the class properties using property drawers and decorator drawer. These require less effort than the inspectors and are applied using attributes.

In the next chapter, we will continue working on the Level Creator using editor windows to create a Piece Palette.

Creating Editor Windows

Most of the interactions you have with Unity when you use the Scene View, Game View, or Project browser will be across editor windows. When you need to have some kind of interaction that is not directly related to one specific object instance, the usage of a editor window feels more natural compared to a custom inspector.

Unity allows you to create editor windows using the `EditorWindow` class, giving you an alternative way to create user interfaces for your tools.

Here, you will learn how to create an editor window and customize it to build a Palette to display the level piece prefabs available in *Run & Jump* in order to be used by the Level Creator.

In this chapter, we will cover the following topics:

- The `EditorWindow` class
- The `AssetDatabase` class
- C# events

Overview

An editor window is used as a base to display the GUI and support all the user interactions for a specific functionality. In Unity, most of the graphical elements you see are rendered over an editor window, and these can float freely or can be docked as a tab; these can be simple or complex depending of what they need to achieve. See the editor window in the following screenshot:

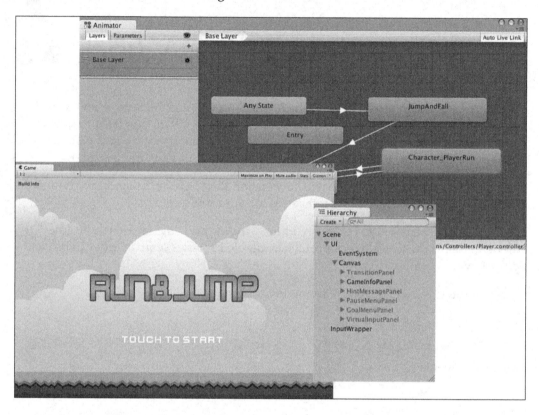

All the editor windows extend from the EditorWindow class, which is to be used in order to create our own custom editor windows.

In this chapter, you will learn how to create a custom editor window implementing a Palette, a window that will display the level piece prefabs of the video game.

Defining the chapter goals

In this chapter, we will improve the way a level designer searches for a level piece prefab to use it on a level in the Level Creator tool. Instead of using the Project browser, we will create a Palette using the `EditorWindow` class.

The goals here are:

- Implementing a category system
- Getting a reference to all the level piece prefabs of the project and categorize them
- Creating a tab system to display categories
- Creating a GUI element to represent the level piece prefab in the Palette
- Creating a scrollable area to display the level piece prefabs
- Integrating the Palette with the Level Creator tool

The final result that we will achieve looks like this:

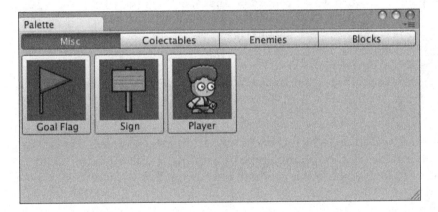

Creating the base for an editor window

In this section, we will create the base code to get an editor window up and running in Unity.

Using the EditorWindow class

The `EditorWindow` class is part of the `UnityEditor` namespace and must be extended to any class used to create editor windows.

 To use the `EditorWindow` class, you must place your script inside an Editor folder, or in a folder nested inside an `Editor` folder.

Create a script called `PaletteWindow.cs` inside the folder `Tools/LevelCreator/Editor`, and then add the following code:

```
using UnityEngine;
using UnityEditor;

namespace RunAndJump.LevelCreator {
  public class PaletteWindow : EditorWindow {

    public static PaletteWindow instance;

    public static void ShowPalette () {
      instance = (PaletteWindow) EditorWindow.GetWindow
(typeof(PaletteWindow));
      instance.titleContent = new GUIContent("Palette");
    }
  }
}
```

The `GetWindow` method, which is part of the `EditorWindow` class, is responsible for getting an instance of the specified type of window, in this case, the `PaletteWindow` type. So, each time you call this method, the current live window instance will be returned.

Here, we created a static method called `ShowPalette`, which encapsulates the `GetWindow` call, and a static variable called `instance` to save the reference to the `PalleteWindow` instance. This follows a singleton pattern.

Finally, we need to call the `ShowPalette` method to display the Palette in the editor. We will use a menu item attribute for this. Go to the `MenuItems.cs` script we created in a preceding chapter and add the following lines of code inside the `MenuItems` class:

```
[MenuItem ("Tools/Level Creator/Show Palette")]
private static void ShowPalette () {
  PaletteWindow.ShowPalette ();
}
```

Save and wait for Unity to compile the scripts. Then, in the Unity editor menu, navigate to **Tools | Level Creator**. Here, you will see a new item called **Show Palette**:

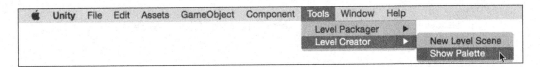

After you click on it, the Palette window instance will appear over the Unity editor:

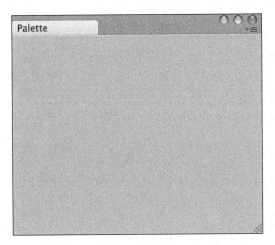

You will notice that the behavior of this is the same as that of the build-in editor windows of Unity, and you can move it around, dock, minimize, maximize, and close it without problems.

Playing with the EditorWindow message methods

In the `EditorWindow` class, you will find the same message methods that we saw when we implemented the custom inspectors in the previous chapter.

Let's update the `PaletteWindow.cs` script:

```
using UnityEngine;
using UnityEditor;

namespace RunAndJump.LevelCreator {
    public class PaletteWindow : EditorWindow {
```

```
        public static PaletteWindow instance;

        public static void ShowPalette () {
            instance = (PaletteWindow) EditorWindow.GetWindow
    (typeof(PaletteWindow));
            instance.titleContent = new GUIContent("Palette");
        }

        private void OnEnable() {
           Debug.Log("OnEnable called...");
        }

        private void OnDisable() {
           Debug.Log("OnDisable called...");
        }

        private void OnDestroy() {
           Debug.Log("OnDestroy called...");
        }

        private void OnGUI() {
            EditorGUILayout.LabelField("The GUI of this window was
    modified.");
        }
    private void Update () {
            // Debug.Log("OnGUI called...");
        }
    }
```

The OnEnable, OnDisable, and OnDestroy methods have the same behavior as
explained in *Chapter 3, Creating Custom Inspectors*.

Inside the OnGUI method, you can add your methods to render the GUI. To see how
it works, we added a label field. This works similar to the OnInspectorGUI method
used for custom inspectors.

There is also a method called Update. This is called 100 times per second in all the
visible windows. We will use this later for a method that requires working in an
asynchronous way.

After saving and waiting for Unity to compile, go to the Level Creator menu and click on **Show Palette**. The Palette window now will show the GUI element that we added in the OnGUI method:

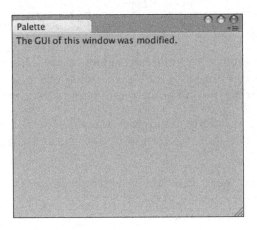

 We limited the methods shown here to the ones we need in the PaletteWindow method, but there are a lot of other functionalities to explore. You can check out more about the EditorWindow class at http://docs.unity3d.com/ScriptReference/ EditorWindow.html.

Using Hotkeys to trigger menu items

When you need to add an entry point to allow people to use your tools, it is a good alternative to create a new menu item in the Unity editor menu so that you can trigger the necessary method to initialize and show your tools with just a click.

The MenuItem attribute allows you to do this. All you need to do is to ensure that you are using the UnityEditor namespace and ensure that the target method is static.

In order to save the users' time, you can assign Hotkeys to menu items. The following table shows the strings that you need to add to the path parameter; use the following specific keys (these can also be combined together):

String	Key
%	*Ctrl* on Windows / *Command* on OSX
#	*Shift*
&	*Alt*

String	Key
LEFT/RIGHT/UP/DOWN	Arrow keys
F1...F2	F keys
HOME, END, PGUP, PGDN	Home, End, Page Up, Page Down

Character keys, which are not part of a key sequence, are added by prefixing them with an underscore (for example, _g for the shortcut key G). The Hotkey character combinations are added to the end of the menu item path, preceded by a space.

We will update the **Show Palette** menu item to make it work with the Hotkey *P* as well. Go to the script `MenuItems.cs` and update the method `ShowPalette`, as follows:

```
[MenuItem ("Tools/Level Creator/Show Palette _p")]
private static void ShowPalette () {
    PaletteWindow.ShowPalette ();
}
```

Now, if you check the **Show Palette** menu item, you will see the letter **P** at the end. This means that you can press *P* on the keyboard and open the Palette window:

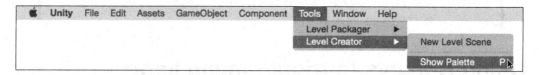

Implementing the Palette

In this section, we will get hands on with the implementation of the Palette. Just to maintain a certain level of abstraction, in some cases, we will talk about Palette items instead level piece prefabs.

For us, a Palette item is what is displayed in the Palette, and this can be anything; in this case, a level piece prefab.

Creating a category system

We need some data to make the Palette window functional. The first step is to categorize the available level piece prefabs in the game. In *Run & Jump*, all the level piece prefabs are located in `Prefabs/LevelPieces`:

We will create a script with a mission to save information about the level piece prefabs, which includes the category. Inside the `Tools/LevelCreator/Scripts` folder, create a script called `PaletteItem.cs` with the following code:

```
using UnityEngine;

namespace RunAndJump.LevelCreator {
    public class PaletteItem: MonoBehaviour {
    #if UNITY_EDITOR
        public enum Category {
            Misc,
            Colectables,
            Enemies,
            Blocks,
        }

        public Category category = Category.Misc;
        public string itemName = "" ;
        public Object inspectedScript;
    #endif
    }
}
```

Save the script, and then attach this script to each level piece prefab. By doing this, each prefab will have the following properties:

- `category`: This is a value from the enum category that defines in which one the level piece prefab will be displayed. The default category is `Misc`.

- `itemName`: This is the name associated to the level piece prefab.

- `inspectedScript`: This is a reference to the script that gives the main behavior to the piece. This will be used to access the specific properties of the level piece prefab later.

As these properties are only necessary in the Editor context, a preprocessor directive using the symbol `UNITY_EDITOR` was added.

The final step here is to fill the fields of the properties in the inspector. As a reference, use the following table:

Prefab	Category	Name	Reference
EnemyYellowFace	Enemies	Angry Blob	`EnemyYellowFaceController.cs`
HazardSpikes	Blocks	Spikes	`HazardSpikesController.cs`
InteractiveCoin	Colectables	Coin	`InteractiveCoinController.cs`
InteractiveGoalFlag	Misc	Goal Flag	`InteractiveGoalFlag.cs`
InteractiveSign	Misc	Sign	`InteractiveSignController.cs`
InteractiveTreasure	Colectables	Treasure	`InteractiveTreasureController.cs`
Player	Misc	Timmy	`PlayerController.cs`
SolidDirt	Blocks	Dirt	`BlockController.cs`
SolidGrass	Blocks	Grass	`BlockController.cs`

At the end, you will have something like this for each level piece prefab:

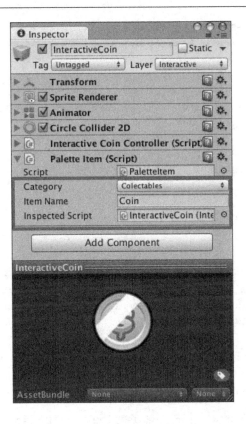

 Don't forget to attach the main script to the **Inspected Script** property!

Finding assets using the AssetDatabase class

To be able to get a reference to all the level pieces in the project, we will create a utility method called `GetAssetsWithScripts` inside the `EditorUtils` class:

```
public static List<T> GetAssetsWithScript<T> (string path) where T :
MonoBehaviour {
    T tmp;
    string assetPath;
    GameObject asset;
```

```
        List<T> assetList = new List<T> ();
        string[] guids = AssetDatabase.FindAssets ("t:Prefab", new
string[] {path});
        for (int i = 0; i < guids.Length; i++) {
          assetPath = AssetDatabase.GUIDToAssetPath (guids [i]);
          asset = AssetDatabase.LoadAssetAtPath (assetPath,
typeof(GameObject)) as GameObject;
          tmp = asset.GetComponent<T> ();
          if (tmp != null) {
            assetList.Add (tmp);
          }
        }
      return assetList;
    }
```

 Here, we use generics to maximize code reuse. Because of this, you must add using `System.Collections.Generic;` to your `EditorUtils` class. To know more about generics, visit `https://msdn.microsoft.com/en-us/library/512aeb7t.aspx`.

This method receives a generic type and a path, and will search all the prefabs relative to the path that has a script corresponding to the generic type attached. The result is a list with all the script instances.

To achieve this, `GetAssetsWithScript` uses the `AssetDatabase` class, part from the `UnityEditor` namespace. This class is used as an interface for accessing assets and performing operations on assets.

The `FindAssets` method searches the asset database using a search filter string and returns a list of GUID. Here, we look for all the assets with the type prefab, and as a second parameter, we focus the search to one specific path (this method accepts an array of paths if you need).

 GUID is an acronym for global unique identifier. This is a number that represents a unique identity for an entity.

With the GUIDs, we use two other methods to get a game object instance of each prefab: `GUIDToAssetPath` and `LoadAssetAtPath`.

Finally, we check whether the game object has the script attached. If the answer is yes, this will be added to the list and returned by the method.

The `AssetDatabase` class is very useful class to deal with the asset management in our project through code. To get more information, visit `http://docs.unity3d.com/ScriptReference/AssetDatabase.html`.

Implementing the GUI for the Palette

In this section, we will add our custom GUI and functionalities to the Palette window.

Creating tabs

We want to use the category names as labels for a set of tabs in the Palette window. When we select one of these tabs, only the level piece prefabs of the selected category will be displayed.

We will create a method called `GetListFromEnum`. This will help us to easily list enums for further use. Let's add this method inside the `EditorUtils` class:

```
public static List<T> GetListFromEnum<T> () {
    List<T> enumList = new List<T> ();
    System.Array enums = System.Enum.GetValues (typeof(T));
    foreach (T e in enums) {
        enumList.Add (e);
    }
    return enumList;
}
```

The method receives an enum type as a generic type and returns a list with all the enum values in it.

Now, to create the GUI for the tabs, we need to make a few updates in the `PaletteWindow.cs` script, as follows:

```
using UnityEngine;
using UnityEditor;
using System.Collections.Generic;

namespace RunAndJump.LevelCreator {
    public class PaletteWindow : EditorWindow {
    private List<PaletteItem.Category> _categories;
    private List<string> _categoryLabels;
```

```
    private PaletteItem.Category _categorySelected;

// Rest of the code...
  }
}
```

Now, we initialize these variables in the OnEnable method:

```
private void OnEnable() {
  if (_categories == null) {
     InitCategories ();
    }
}

private void InitCategories () {
  Debug.Log ("InitCategories called...");
  _categories = EditorUtils.GetListFromEnum<PaletteItem.Category> ();
  _categoryLabels = new List<string> ();
  foreach (PaletteItem.Category category in _categories) {
    _categoryLabels.Add (category.ToString ());
  }
}
```

Here, we get and save the categories using a string array; this will be used to set up the labels of the tabs.

Create a new method called DrawTabs and add the following:

```
private void DrawTabs () {
    int index = (int)_categorySelected;
    index = GUILayout.Toolbar (index, _categoryLabels.ToArray ());
    _categorySelected = _categories [index];
  }
```

Here, we use the class GUI to render a toolbar. This GUI component is an array of buttons; depending on the button you press, the number representing that button is returned.

Now, let's add a reference of this method inside the OnGUI method:

```
private void OnGUI() {
    DrawTabs();
  }
```

Now, save and wait for Unity to compile. If the Palette window is open, close it. Then, go to the Level Creator menu and click on **Show Palette**.

You will see the following:

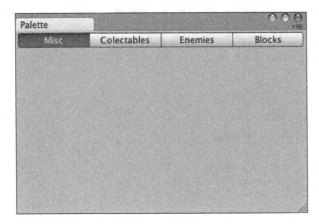

You will see the tabs working, and each time you press a tab, the category is saved in the variable `_categorySelected`.

Creating a scrollable area

In the space we are not using for the tabs, we will present all the available level piece prefabs of the selected category. As the number of prefabs can be huge, we will model this as a scrollable area.

Before we create the scrollable area, we need to define a few variables inside the `PaletteWindow` class:

```
private string _path = "Assets/Prefabs/LevelPieces";
private List<PaletteItem> _items;
private Dictionary<PaletteItem.Category, List<PaletteItem>> _
categorizedItems;
private Dictionary<PaletteItem, Texture2D> _previews;
private Vector2 _scrollPosition;
private const float ButtonWidth = 80;
private const float ButtonHeight = 90;
```

The `_path` variable defines where the Palette window will search the level piece prefabs. In this case, we will in `Assets/Prefabs/LevelPieces`.

We also created two dictionaries, which are as follows:

- `_categorizedItems`: This is where the keys are the category and the values are lists of the `PaletteItem` class instances
- `_previews`: This is where the keys are the `PaletteItem` class and the value is a Texture2D that represents the preview of the item

Again, all the initialization will occur inside the `OnEnable` method:

```
private void OnEnable () {
    // Debug.Log("OnEnable called...");
    if (_categories == null) {
        InitCategories ();
    }
    if (_categorizedItems == null) {
        InitContent ();
    }
}
private void InitContent () {
    Debug.Log ("InitContent called...");
    // Set the ScrollList
    _items = EditorUtils.GetAssetsWithScript<PaletteItem> (_path);
    _categorizedItems = new Dictionary<PaletteItem.Category,
List<PaletteItem>> ();
    _previews = new Dictionary<PaletteItem, Texture2D> ();
    // Init the Dictionary
    foreach (PaletteItem.Category category in _categories) {
        _categorizedItems.Add (category, new List<PaletteItem> ());
    }
    // Assign items to each category
    foreach (PaletteItem item in _items) {
        _categorizedItems [item.category].Add (item);
    }
}
```

To explain how to implement the scrollable area, we will use a top-down approach. So, let's start by defining the method responsible for drawing this. Create a method called `DrawScroll` and add the following code:

```
private void DrawScroll () {
    if (_categorizedItems [_categorySelected].Count == 0) {
        EditorGUILayout.HelpBox ("This category is empty!",
MessageType.Info);
```

```
        return;
    }
    int rowCapacity =
        Mathf.FloorToInt (position.width / (ButtonWidth));
    _scrollPosition =
        GUILayout.BeginScrollView (_scrollPosition);
    int selectionGridIndex = -1;
    selectionGridIndex = GUILayout.SelectionGrid (
        selectionGridIndex,
        GetGUIContentsFromItems (),
        rowCapacity,
        GetGUIStyle ());
    GetSelectedItem (selectionGridIndex);
    GUILayout.EndScrollView ();
}
```

In this method, we first check whether the current category has level piece prefabs, if isn't, a text **This category is empty** is displayed.

To render a grid of elements inside a scrollable area, we use the following methods:

- `BeginScrollView` and `EndScrollView`: These methods are used to define the scrollable area

- `SelectionGrid`: This method is used to generate a grid of buttons

By default, the `SelectionGrid` method creates a group of buttons that behaves like toggle buttons and the index (from 0 to n-1, where n is the total of elements) of the button selected is returned. To avoid the toggle behavior, we always clean the index returned. So, we save the result in the `selectionGridIndex` variable, but we always set this to -1 before passing it again to the method.

We are going to use the class `AssetPreview`, part of the `UnityEditor` namespace, to automatically create the previews of the level piece prefabs.

The `GetAssetPreview` method returns a Texture2D representing the preview of a game object. This means that if the game object changes, its representation in the Palette will change too.

Add a new method called `GeneratePreviews` with the following code:

```
private void GeneratePreviews () {
    foreach (PaletteItem item in _items) {
        if (!_previews.ContainsKey (item)) {
            Texture2D preview = AssetPreview.GetAssetPreview (item.
gameObject);
```

```
        if (preview != null) {
          _previews.Add (item, preview);
      }
    }
  }
}
```

This preceding code could be called in the `OnEnable` method; the problem appears when you restart Unity. In this process, all the previews are generated in the Unity editor and there is a huge probability that the previews won't be available when you call the `OnEnable` method.

It's because of this that we will place the `GeneratePreviews` method inside the `Update` method, checking constantly until we get the previews. The following is the `Update` method:

```
private void Update () {
        if (_previews.Count != _items.Count) {
            GeneratePreviews ();
        }
    }
```

> To get more information about the `AssetPreview` class, visit `http://docs.unity3d.com/ScriptReference/AssetPreview.html`.

To define the elements of the `SelectionGrid` GUI, we created two auxiliary methods in the `PaletteWindow` class. The first method is `GetGUIContentsFromItems`, as shown in the following code:

```
private GUIContent[] GetGUIContentsFromItems () {
    List<GUIContent> guiContents = new List<GUIContent> ();
    if(_previews.Count == _items.Count) {
        int totalItems = _categorizedItems [_categorySelected].Count;
        for (int i = 0; i < totalItems; i ++) {
            GUIContent guiContent = new GUIContent ();
            guiContent.text = _categorizedItems [_categorySelected]
[i].itemName;
            guiContent.image = _previews [_categorizedItems [_
categorySelected] [i]];
            guiContents.Add (guiContent);
        }
    }
    return guiContents.ToArray ();
}
```

We use a `GUIContent` object to create a button that have with the label and an image. The data for the label comes from the `PaletteItem` class and the image from the dictionary that we created in the `OnEnable` method.

This method takes care of including in the array only the `GUIContent` instances related to the level pieces prefabs available in the current category.

The second auxiliary method is `GetGUIStyle`, as shown in the following code:

```
private GUIStyle GetGUIStyle () {
        GUIStyle guiStyle = new GUIStyle (GUI.skin.button);
        guiStyle.alignment = TextAnchor.LowerCenter;
        guiStyle.imagePosition = ImagePosition.ImageAbove;
        guiStyle.fixedWidth = ButtonWidth;
        guiStyle.fixedHeight = ButtonHeight;
        return guiStyle;
    }
```

We use an instance of the class `GUIStyle` parameter to change how the button looks (we will talk more about this in *Chapter 6, Changing the Look and Feel of the Editor with GUI Styles and GUI Skins*).

By default, a button will place the label and image, respectively, in a horizontal way. Here, we change this to place the image over the label and also to centrally align the text of that label.

Finally, in order to know which piece was selected in the Palette, we created a method called `GetSelectedItem` that converts the index returned by the `SelectionGrid` GUI component to a level piece:

```
private void GetSelectedItem (int index) {
            if (index != -1) {
                PaletteItem selectedItem =
                    _categorizedItems [_categorySelected] [index];
                Debug.Log ("Selected Item is: " +
                    selectedItem.itemName);
    }
```

Now, the last thing to do is to add `DrawScroll` to the `OnGUI` method:

```
private void OnGUI() {
        DrawTabs();
        DrawScroll();
    }
```

After saving and waiting for Unity to compile, go to the **Level Creator** menu and click on **Show Palette** (if the Palette is open, close it and open it again):

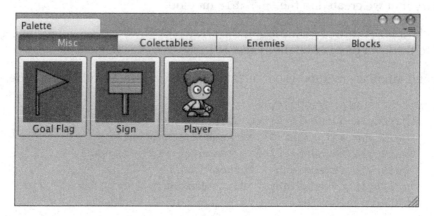

Now, all the level pieces inside the path Assets/Prefabs/LevelPieces appear in the Palette. You don't need to navigate across the project hierarchy to find them. If you click on a tab, only the pieces of that category are displayed.

If you select a category without level pieces, you will see something like this:

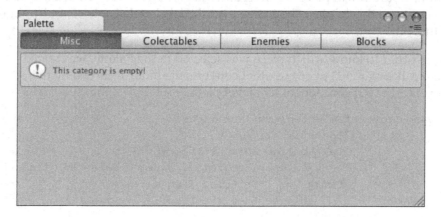

A text indicates that the category is empty. Now, if we change the category of all the level pieces to Misc, we will see a crowd category, but the scroll area handles the overflow adding a scrollbar to navigate:

We have the Palette window up and running. Now, we need to integrate this to the rest of the Level Creator tool. In the final part of this chapter, we will work on the integration of this editor window with the custom inspector we created in the previous chapter.

Integrating the Palette with the Level Creator tool

In this section, we will create an event that will be triggered every time you select a piece in the Palette and captured by the Level inspector. This feature will be used in the next chapter.

Creating an event

An event in C# is a way for a class to provide notifications when something happens to an object.

In this case, we will add an event when the user selects one of the pieces from the Palette. To achieve this, we we will add the following lines of code to the `PalleteWindow.cs` script:

```
public delegate void itemSelectedDelegate (PaletteItem item, Texture2D
preview);
public static event itemSelectedDelegate ItemSelectedEvent;
```

The `delegate` type defines the signature for the method that handles the event. In this case, `itemSelectedDelegate` receives a PaletteItem and a Texture2D with the preview.

 As a good practice, it is always recommended to check if the even is, or is not, null.

Now, it is time to invoke the event. We will do this inside the `GetSelectedItem` method:

```
private void GetSelectedItem (int index) {
  if (index != -1) {
    PaletteItem selectedItem =
          _categorizedItems [_categorySelected] [index];
    Debug.Log ("Selected Item is: " +
      selectedItem.itemName);

    if (ItemSelectedEvent != null) {
      ItemSelectedEvent (selectedItem, _previews [selectedItem]);
    }
  }
}
```

We are done here. Now, we need to subscribe to this event in the Level inspector class.

Subscribing to an event

Now, we will subscribe to the event we created. This is done with the `+=` and `-=` operators, which are used to subscribe and unsubscribe respectively.

Before adding the events, we will create the variables and methods that we need to make this work. The plan is to display the selected piece in the inspector. We will add a variable to save the selected piece instance in the `LevelInspector.cs` script:

```
using UnityEngine;
using UnityEditor;

namespace RunAndJump.LevelCreator {
    [CustomEditor(typeof(Level))]
```

```
public class LevelInspector : Editor {

    private PaletteItem _itemSelected;
    private Texture2D _itemPreview;
    private LevelPiece _pieceSelected;

    // Rest of the code...
    }
}
```

We will create the method that we want to subscribe to the event called
UpdateCurrentPieceInstance:

```
private void UpdateCurrentPieceInstance(PaletteItem item, Texture2D
preview) {
    _itemSelected = item;
    _itemPreview = preview;
    _pieceSelected = (LevelPiece) item.GetComponent<LevelPiece>();
    Repaint();
}
```

When the event is triggered, the piece selected will be passed as a parameter and
saved in _pieceSelected. As we want to see a few changes in the inspector when
this happens, we also use the method Repaint to force the inspector to repaint.

To subscribe and unsubscribe from this event, we will use the OnEnable and
OnDisable methods respectively:

```
private void OnEnable () {
    _myTarget = (Level)target;
    InitLevel ();
    ResetResizeValues ();
    SubscribeEvents();
}

private void OnDisable () {
    UnsubscribeEvents();
}
private void SubscribeEvents() {
    PaletteWindow.ItemSelectedEvent += new PaletteWindow.itemSelectedD
elegate(UpdateCurrentPieceInstance);
}

private void UnsubscribeEvents() {
```

```
        PaletteWindow.ItemSelectedEvent -= new PaletteWindow.
    itemSelectedDelegate( UpdateCurrentPieceInstance);
    }
```

With this, we have all the necessary logic implemented. The last thing to conclude is to see something in the inspector. For this, create a new method called DrawPieceSelectedGUI:

```
    private void DrawPieceSelectedGUI() {
        EditorGUILayout.LabelField("Piece Selected", EditorStyles.
    boldLabel);
        if(_pieceSelected == null) {
            EditorGUILayout.HelpBox("No piece selected!", MessageType.
    Info);
        } else {
            EditorGUILayout.BeginVertical("box");
            EditorGUILayout.LabelField(new GUIContent(_itemPreview),
    GUILayout.Height(40));
            EditorGUILayout.LabelField(_itemSelected.itemName);
            EditorGUILayout.EndVertical();
        }
    }
```

Now, add DrawPieceSelectedGUI to the OnInspectorGUI method:

```
    public override void OnInspectorGUI () {
      // DrawDefaultInspector();
        DrawLevelDataGUI ();
        DrawLevelSizeGUI ();
        DrawPieceSelectedGUI();

        if (GUI.changed) {
          EditorUtility.SetDirty (_myTarget);
        }
    }
```

We are ready to do the final test. After saving and waiting for Unity to compile, create a new level and display the Palette window using the Level Creator menu:

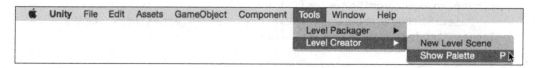

Now, you will see something like this:

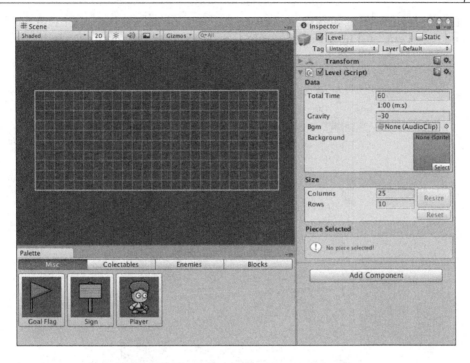

If you pay attention to the inspector, there is a new label that says **No piece selected!**, as you can see in the following screenshot:

Select the category **Misc**, and then click on the **Sign** piece; the Inspector will be listened the event, and now Piece Selected section shows the piece selected:

With this working, we are ready to implement, in the next chapter, the functionality of adding pieces to the scene to start creating levels for *Run & Jump*. Good work!

Summary

In this chapter, you learned about how to implement editor windows to create a new way to interact with our tools.

The `EditorWindow` class is part of the `UnityEditor` namespace and it is necessary to extend from that to create your own editor window. You must save your editor window class inside an `Editor` folder to make it work.

A big challenge in the creation of the editor window is to define the approach to create a GUI. You can use layouts if you use methods from `EditorGUILayout` and `GUILayout`, or take care of the position of each component using a Rect approach, which means using methods from `EditorGUI` and GUI. The best advice you can get here is to not be afraid of jumping around all the different classes to create your GUI.

Using an editor window or an inspector will depend of your design. Remember, the inspector was designed to expose parameters from a specific element. A window is more generic and doesn't require an inspected element to work.

In the next chapter, we will continue working in the Level Creator tool, focusing on the customization the Scene View. We will finally implement functionalities to start adding content to the level.

5

Customizing the Scene View

Unity's component system and also the ability it offers to see the scene you are building in real time makes it very easy to work with. The Scene View in Unity provides the tools to interact with all the objects of the scene, and also offers the ability to navigate between them just to check whether everything is place.

There are a few `Editor` classes that allow you to interact with the Scene View through code, offering the ability to make customizations. Understanding how to achieve these kinds of things is very important when you start creating more interactive and complex tools for your video game projects.

Here we are going to learn how to customize the Scene View to make it suitable for our Level Creator tool requirements, such as creating, editing, and deleting level piece prefabs from the level scene.

In this chapter, we will cover the following topics:

- The `OnSceneGUI` message method
- Adding a GUI
- Events
- Handles
- Hiding flags

Overview

The Scene View is an editor window that allows you to look around your game scene and manipulate its contents. The following screenshot illustrates the Scene View:

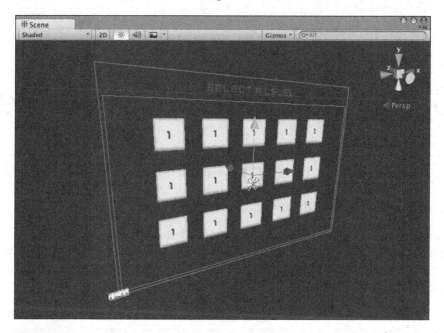

At this point you know that almost everything in Unity is customizable, and the Scene View is no exception.

In this chapter, we will cover how to add GUI to the Scene View and change the common behavior it has to make it work specifically for our Level Creator tool.

Defining the chapter goals

In this chapter we want to customize the Scene View to follow the workflow of the Level Creator tool, this means the user is capable of viewing the level and adding, deleting, and editing level piece prefabs.

The goals here are:

- Defining the Level Creator interaction modes
- Adding the necessary GUI to support the mode selection
- Capturing mouse events
- Implementing the functionality of each mode

The final result that we will achieve looks like this:

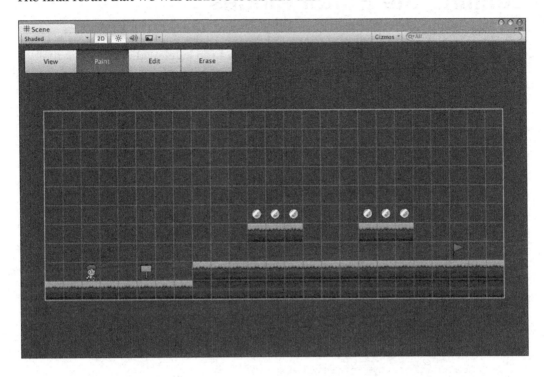

As we mentioned in *Chapter 2, Using Gizmos in the Scene View*, we will assume that the Level game object position and rotation are (0,0,0) and the scale is (1,1,1) always. Also, 2D mode is selected by default. In this chapter we are going to implement ways to keep these restrictions by code, but until that happens, be sure you respect these in order to test the rest of the code.

If you have problems with the code, remember always to create a new level scene before testing the changes. This is because errors can sometimes corrupt data at the stage we are currently at.

Defining the Editor modes

The Level Creator tool is going to have four different modes:

- **View**: You can move, orbit, or zoom around the level grid. This is just the default behavior Unity has when you select the hand tool.

- **Paint**: By clicking or dragging the mouse on the level grid, you can add level piece prefabs to it. The piece you will be "painting" in the level grid is the one you selected on the Palette window.

- **Edit**: By clicking on a piece from the level grid you can access its properties in the Level Inspector and make tweaks to it if necessary.

- **Erase**: By clicking or dragging the mouse on the level grid over existing pieces, you can remove them.

In the LevelInspector class, we are going to add an enum to list these modes and a variable to save the one that is currently active:

```
using UnityEngine;
using UnityEditor;

using System.Collections.Generic;

namespace RunAndJump.LevelCreator {
    [CustomEditor(typeof(Level))]
    public class LevelInspector : Editor {

        public enum Mode {
            View,
            Paint,
            Edit,
            Erase,
        }

        private Mode _selectedMode;
        private Mode _currentMode;

        // rest of the code
    }
}
```

By default, the selected mode will be the View mode.

Later on in this chapter, we will take care of the implementation of these. For now let's focus on how to switch between modes.

 We added the line using System.Collections.Generic; to the class because we are going to make use of generic collection types, such as lists, later.

Customizing the Scene View

In this section we are going to take a look how to create a custom GUI in the Scene View and change its default behavior.

Using the OnSeceneGUI message method

To start rendering a GUI in Scene View, we are going to make use of a message method part of the Editor class, OnSeceneGUI.

In terms of GUI creation, we can make use of all the techniques we learned in the previous chapters working with custom inspectors and editor windows. In this case, we are going to use a toolbar component like the one used in the Palette window to simulate the tabs.

To see how this works, we are going to create a toolbar attached to the left top corner of the scene view. Each item of this toolbar will be one of the possible modes.

Let's add this method with the following code inside the LevelInspector class:

```
private void DrawModeGUI() {
    List<Mode> modes = EditorUtils.GetListFromEnum<Mode>();
    List<string> modeLabels = new List<string>();
    foreach(Mode mode in modes) {
        modeLabels.Add(mode.ToString());
    }

    Handles.BeginGUI();

    GUILayout.BeginArea(new Rect(10f, 10f, 360, 40f));
    _selectedMode = (Mode) GUILayout.Toolbar(
        (int) _currentMode,
        modeLabels.ToArray(),
        GUILayout.ExpandHeight(true));
    GUILayout.EndArea();

    Handles.EndGUI();

}
```

Then, let's add the `OnSceneGUI` method and call `EditorModeGUI` method from there:

```
private void OnSceneGUI() {
    DrawModeGUI();
}
```

`OnSceneGUI` is a method that handles the events from the Scene View. Here you can add your custom GUI with the help of the class `Handles`. You must place your GUI code between the methods `BeginGUI` and `EndGUI` (the ones highlighted) to see it rendered in the Scene View.

We used the methods `BeginArea` and `EndArea` just to set the boundaries of the place for the layout methods we are going to be using. If you don't do this, all the GUI elements will be adjusted based on the Scene View size.

Save the changes and wait for Unity to compile. Now create a new level by going to **Tools | Level Creator | New Level Scene**:

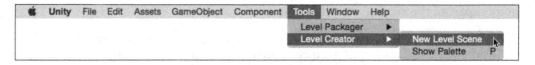

Select the `Level` game object and you will see the toolbar GUI in the top-left corner of the Scene View:

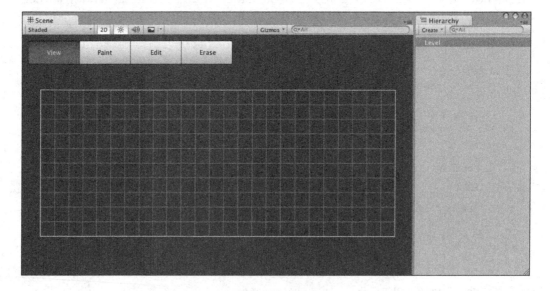

Something you may have noticed is that we aren't saving the value returned by GUILayout.Toolbar in _currentMode; instead, we are using a second variable called _selectedMode. We are going to use these two variables to detect when the current mode changes.

For now, this makes it impossible to change the current selection of the toolbar.

Playing with the Scene View tools

In the top part of the editor, you will find the Unity Toolbar, a set of controls related to different parts of the Unity editor:

On the left are the Transform tools, which define how the interaction with the different game objects inside the Scene View will be. They are shown in the following screenshot:

Here you can choose, from left to right, whether you want to view, move, rotate, or scale game objects or deal with 2D Rects.

For our purposes, we want to choose when the Transform Tools are or are not activated based on the current Level Creator mode. For example, we don't want to rotate a piece by accident when we are painting pieces on the level grid.

To do this, we are going to use the class Tool, part of the UnityEditor namespace, to manipulate the activated tool in the Scene View.

Let's add this method with the following code inside the `LevelInspector` class:

```
private void ModeHandler () {
  switch (_selectedMode) {
    case Mode.Paint:
    case Mode.Edit:
    case Mode.Erase:
       Tools.current = Tool.None;
      break;
    case Mode.View:
    default:
       Tools.current = Tool.View;
      break;
  }
  // Detect Mode change
    if(_selectedMode != _currentMode) {
      _currentMode = _selectedMode;
  }
  // Force 2D Mode!
  SceneView.currentDrawingSceneView.in2DMode = true;
}
```

The variable `current` from the class `Tools` has the information about the current tool selected in the editor. It is possible to overwrite its value using one of the available options in the `Tool` enum. The possible values are:

- Move
- Rotate
- Scale
- Rect
- None

In the `ModeHandler` method we set `Tool.View` for when the Level Creator View mode is selected; otherwise, `Tool.None` is defined.

Here we compare the variables `_currentMode` and `_selectedMode` to check for a mode change; if this happens, we save the value in `_currentMode` . Later, we are going to add a few other lines to complete the Level Creator tool.

At the end, we also force the view mode of the scene to 2D. You are going to notice the 2D button is always pressed.

Finally, call the `EditorModeHandler` function from inside the `OnSceneGUI` method:

```
private void OnSceneGUI() {
  DrawModeGUI();
  ModeHandler();
}
```

Save the changes and wait for Unity to compile. Now create a level, select the game object, and then check Level Creator; the **View** mode is selected:

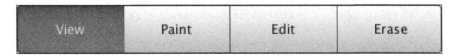

Independent of the Transform Tool selected on Unity, when the Level Creator View mode is selected, the Transform Tool changes to the Unity View tool. In fact, if you try to change the current Transform Tool manually, the code we created overwrites your choice. If you try the same with the **Paint**, **Edit** or **Erase** Level Creator modes, no Transform Tool is selected.

Controlling the focus over our game objects

By default, each time you click on a game object in the Scene View, this one will get focused; if you click on the Scene View directly, the current game object will lose focus.

In Level Creator, if you select a mode different from **View**, let's say **Paint**, clicking in any part of the Scene View makes you lose focus of the level game object and the GUI disappears (remember that the code for the Scene View GUI is on the custom inspector script):

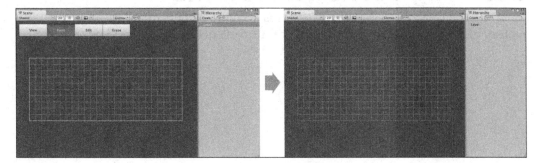

This happens because, when you use a Transform Tool different from `Tool.View` (and this includes `Tool.None`), a click on the Scene View changes the focus of the current game object selected. For the **Paint**, **Edit** and **Erase** Level Creator modes, we need to use the mouse to do the interaction, and this means a lot of clicks here and there. We need to find a way to keep the focus over the Level game object artificially.

Let's add this method with the following code inside the `LevelInspector` class:

```
private void EventHandler() {
  HandleUtility.AddDefaultControl(
    GUIUtility.GetControlID(FocusType.Passive));
}
```

Here we are using the class `HandleUtility`, part of the `UnityEditor` namespace. With `FocusType.Passive`, we are setting the Scene View to a passive mode. This means we need to take care of all the interactivity by our selfs instead of delegating this to Unity.

Then call the `EventHandler` function from inside the `OnSceneGUI` method:

```
private void OnSceneGUI() {
    DrawModeGUI();
    ModeHandler();
    EventHandler();
}
```

Save the changes and wait for Unity to compile. If you repeat the same experiment, you will notice you can't change the focus of the objects by making mouse clicks any more.

Detecting Scene View events

Most of the interaction with Level Creator is going to be performed through the mouse. In this section, will learn how to capture events in the Scene View.

Getting the mouse position

The Event class, part of the UnityEngine namespace, allows you to handle user inputs such as key presses or mouse actions.

Let's update the method EventHandler inside the LevelInspector class:

```
private void EventHandler() {
    HandleUtility.AddDefaultControl(
    GUIUtility.GetControlID(FocusType.Passive));

    Vector3 mousePosition = Event.current.mousePosition;
    Debug.LogFormat("MousePos: {0}", mousePosition);
}
```

The variable Event.current has the information about the current event that's being processed in the Scene View.

From current, we are accessing the variable mousePosition to determine in which X and Y positions, relative to the Scene View coordinate system, the cursor of the mouse is found.

Save the changes and wait for Unity to compile. Now create a new level scene, select the game object, and then move the mouse over the Scene View. In the console, you will see the logs with the mouse position:

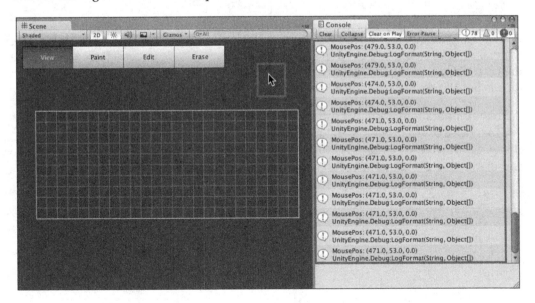

We need to associate the current mouse position with a cell in the grid; this means we transform the mouse position to world coordinates and then to grid coordinates. To achieve this, we will use the method `WorldToGridCoordinates` from the Level class we implemented in *Chapter 2, Using Gizmos in the Scene View*. Let's update the method `EventHandler` again:

```
private void EventHandler() {
    HandleUtility.AddDefaultControl(
    GUIUtility.GetControlID(FocusType.Passive));

    Camera camera =
    SceneView.currentDrawingSceneView.camera;

    Vector3 mousePosition = Event.current.mousePosition;

    //Debug.LogFormat("MousePos: {0}", mousePosition);
    Vector3 worldPos =
    camera.ScreenToWorldPoint(mousePosition);
    Vector3 gridPos =
    _myTarget.WorldToGridCoordinates(worldPos);
    int col = (int) gridPos.x;
    int row = (int) gridPos.y;

    Debug.LogFormat("GridPos {0},{1}", col, row);
}
```

The `SceneView` class is the one that defines the behavior of a Scene View window in Unity. From this class, we used the property `currentDrawingSceneView` to access the current Scene View instance and then to the camera that is rendering the scene (this is not the same camera you use to render in the video game).

With the camera reference, we can use the methods `ScreenToWorldPoint` and `WorldToGridCoordinates` to get column and row grid coordinates. Save the changes and wait for Unity to compile. Now create a level, select the game object, and then move the mouse over the bottom right cell in the grid:

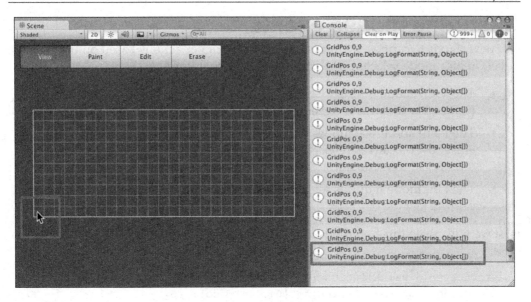

The coordinates of the bottom-left cell are different from the expected (0,0), this happens because the method ScreenToWorldPoint assumes the bottom-left of the screen is *(0,0)* but the Scene View has the origin in the top-left corner.

To solve this, we need to invert the Y-axis of the mouse position. Let's fix the method EventHandler making an adjust in the variable mousePosition, after the line:

```
Vector3 mousePosition = Event.current.mousePosition;
```

Add the following line:

```
mousePosition = new Vector2(mousePosition.x, camera.pixelHeight -
mousePosition.y);
```

Try again; the grid coordinates work perfectly and now we are ready to deal with mouse events.

Capturing mouse events

The next step is to capture the mouse events and trigger actions based on the current Level Creator mode selected. Let's take a look at the following:

- The View mode is already resolved and Unity takes care of that behavior (remember that this is the equivalent to selecting the View Transform Tool)

- The Paint and Erase modes will behave similarly to dragging a pen or an eraser over a canvas respectively, so in this case we want to capture the OnClick() and OnDrag() events

- The Edit mode requires selecting a piece to work, so in this case we want to capture just the OnClick() event

First we will create three methods to handle the modes inside the LevelInspector class:

```
private void Paint(int col, int row) {
    Debug.LogFormat("Painting {0},{1}", col, row);
}
private void Erase(int col, int row) {
    Debug.LogFormat("Erasing {0},{1}", col, row);
}
private void Edit(int col, int row) {
    Debug.LogFormat("Editing {0},{1}", col, row);
}
```

For each mode we will require the grid coordinates as a parameter, and for now, we are going to print a log when any of them is used. Then we will update the EventHandler class to support the mouse events each mode requires, adding the following block of code at the end of this method:

```
switch(_currentMode) {
case Mode.Paint:
  if(Event.current.type == EventType.MouseDown ||
     Event.current.type == EventType.MouseDrag) {
    Paint(col, row);
  }
  break;
case Mode.Edit:
  if(Event.current.type == EventType.MouseDown) {
    Edit(col, row);
    }
```

```
      break;
  case Mode.Erase:
    if(Event.current.type == EventType.MouseDown ||
       Event.current.type == EventType.MouseDrag) {
      Erase(col, row);
    }
    break;
  case Mode.View:
  default:
    break;
  }
```

From `Event.current`, we are using the property type to find which kind of event was triggered in the Scene View.

For each mode, we are comparing the variable `current` with the `MouseDown` or `MouseDrag` event types. For more types of events, you can check the `EventType` enum.

Save the changes and wait for Unity to compile. Now create a level, select the game object, and then with the **Paint** mode selected, click and drag the mouse over the Scene View. Let's take a look at the following screenshot:

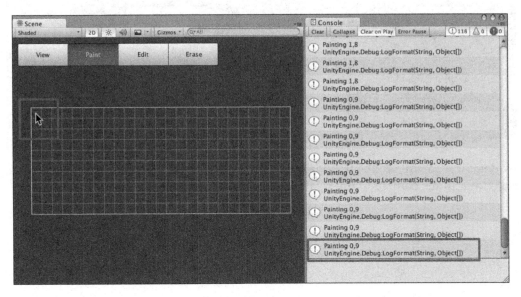

You will see the log of the `Paint` method any time you click or drag the mouse. The same happens with the **Erase** mode, and in the case of the **Edit** mode, this just happens when you click.

At this point, we have most of the interactions ready. It's time to work in the features that will make Level Creator capable of creating content. In the next section, we will implement the Level Creator modes.

Implementing the Level Creator modes

Until this point, we have specified the four modes the Level Creator tool would support and a way to switch between modes, thanks to the custom GUI we added in the top-left corner of the Scene View.

In this section, we discuss how to implement each of them.

The View mode

When you select **View** on Level Creator, you can move or zoom around the level grid.

In the method `ModeHandler` we defined, this mode will behave like the Unity View Transform tool. Let's take a look at following screenshot:

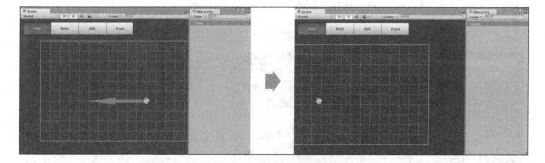

By default, you will see the hand icon on this mode; by clicking and dragging, you can move all the content in the Scene View.

The Paint mode

We started implementing part of the workflow related to this mode in the previous chapters. When this mode is selected, the user must select a piece from the Palette window, and a reference to this selection will be saved in the variable _pieceSelected in the LevelInspector class.

When the user starts clicking and dragging the mouse over the grid, a copy of the level piece prefab will be added to the level. This will be the responsibility of the Paint method.

Let's update that:

```
private void Paint(int col, int row) {
  // Check out of bounds and if we have a piece selected
  if(!_myTarget.IsInsideGridBounds(col,row) ||  _pieceSelected ==
  null) {
    return;
  }
  // Check if I need to destroy a previous piece
  if(_myTarget.Pieces[col + row * _myTarget.TotalColumns] != null)
  {
    DestroyImmediate(_myTarget.Pieces[col + row *
    _myTarget.TotalColumns].gameObject);
  }
  // Do paint !
  GameObject obj = PrefabUtility.InstantiatePrefab(
  _pieceSelected.gameObject) as GameObject;
  obj.transform.parent = _myTarget.transform;
  obj.name = string.Format("[{0},{1}] [{2}]", col, row, obj.name);
  obj.transform.position = _myTarget.GridToWorldCoordinates(col,
  row);
  _myTarget.Pieces[col + row * _myTarget.TotalColumns] =
  obj.GetComponent<LevelPiece>();
}
```

In this method, we first check whether the coordinates for the column and row are inside the grid and whether we have a level piece prefab selected from the Palette window. Then, if the current cell on the grid has something, we destroy that piece using the method DestroyImmediate.

Finally, we proceed to create a copy of the piece in the column and row grid coordinates. To achieve this, we use the `PrefabUtility` class, part of the `UnityEditor` namespace, and the method `InstantiatePrefab`. We are using this class because we want to keep the prefab reference, so if in the future you update the level piece prefabs, with an art change for example, this will be replicated in all the levels.

It's time to test. Save the changes and wait for unity to compile. Create a new level, and also in the Level Creator menu item, select **Show Palette** as shown in the following screenshot:

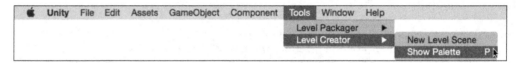

In the Palette window, select the category **Blocks** and then select **Grass**. You will have something like this:

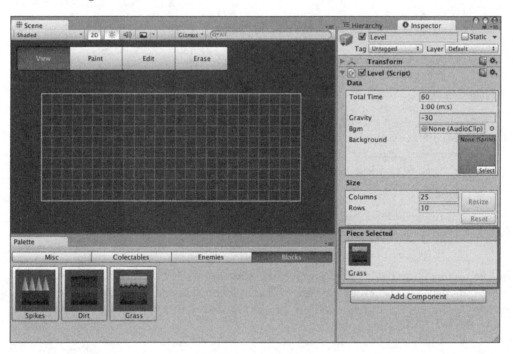

Now, select the **Paint** mode and start clicking and dragging the mouse over the grid. You are finally creating content with Level Creator!

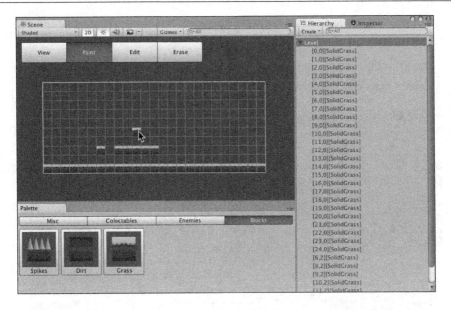

The Erase mode

We are human beings, so we need to accept that we are not perfect and it's because of this that the Erase mode is necessary in the Level Creator tool. This will be the responsibility of the Erase method inside the LevelInspector class.

```
private void Erase(int col, int row) {
    // Check out of bounds
    if(!_myTarget.IsInsideGridBounds(col,row)) {
        return;
    }
    // Do Erase
    if(_myTarget.Pieces[col + row * _myTarget.TotalColumns] !=
null) {
        DestroyImmediate(_myTarget.Pieces[col + row *
        _myTarget.TotalColumns].gameObject);
    }
}
```

This method is very simple. We check whether the coordinates for the column and row are inside the grid, and if the cell contains a piece, we remove that using the DestroyImmediate method.

To test this, save the changes and wait for Unity to compile; then repeat the process for testing the Paint method (but this time fill the whole grid with different pieces).

Now, select the **Erase** mode and start clicking and dragging the mouse over the grid. You will start erasing pieces from the grid.

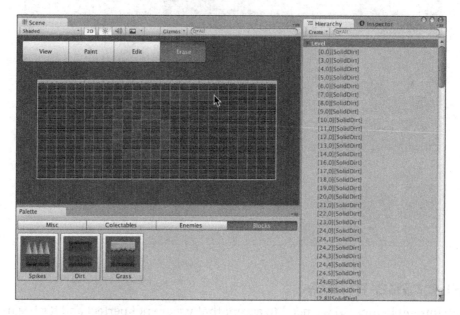

The Edit mode

In Run & Jump, there are a few pieces that receive parameters using the inspector. A good example of this is the **InteractiveSign** piece shown here:

The `InteractiveSignController` script, responsible for the logic for the Sign level piece prefab, has a field called `Message`, a string that is displayed in the video game as follows:

Right now, the way to customize these prefabs is by expanding the level game object in the hierarchy window and finding the specific sign piece game object.

To make this process simpler, we will use the Edit mode. In this mode, when you select one of the pieces of the level, the inspector of that level piece prefab is going to be rendered inside the Level Inspector. This is another example of the flexibility Unity offers to customize the editor to our needs.

Let's update the `Edit` method inside the `LevelInspector` class:

```
private PaletteItem _itemInspected;

private void Edit(int col, int row) {
  // Check out of bounds
  if (!_myTarget.IsInsideGridBounds(col,row) ||
  _myTarget.Pieces[col + row * _myTarget.TotalColumns] ==
  null) {
    _itemInspected = null;
  } else {
    _itemInspected = _myTarget.Pieces[col + row *
    _myTarget.TotalColumns].GetComponent<PaletteItem>() as
    PaletteItem;
  }
  Repaint();
}
```

We created a variable called _itemInspected to save a reference to the piece selected in Edit mode. Then the Edit method took care of checking whether the column and row are inside the grid and if the cell contains a piece. If this is true, the piece is assigned to _itemInspected.

At the end, we added the method Repaint in order to force the Level Inspector to repaint every time we use this method. So if we select a level piece prefab, the inspector will be rendered automatically. We need to create a method responsible for rendering this, so we create a new method called DrawInspectedItemGUI:

```
private void DrawInspectedItemGUI() {
  // Only show this GUI if we are in edit mode.
  if(_currentMode != Mode.Edit) {
    return;
  }

  //EditorGUILayout.LabelField ("Piece Edited", _titleStyle);
  EditorGUILayout.LabelField ("Piece Edited",
  EditorStyles.boldLabel);

  if(_itemInspected != null) {
    EditorGUILayout.BeginVertical("box");
    EditorGUILayout.LabelField("Name: " + _itemInspected.name);
    Editor.CreateEditor(
    _itemInspected.inspectedScript).OnInspectorGUI();
    EditorGUILayout.EndVertical();
  } else {
    EditorGUILayout.HelpBox("No piece to edit!",
    MessageType.Info);
  }
}
```

In the previous chapter, we associated a PaletteItem.cs script with each level piece on the project. One of the fields of this script is called inspectedScript; it is basically the reference to the main script of each level piece prefab. For example, in the case of InteractiveSign, this is the InteractiveSignController script.

The most important thing here is the usage of the method CreateEditor from the class Editor. This creates a custom editor for the target object you pass as a parameter. Then we access to the method OnInspectorGUI of that target object. This opens the possibility of rendering an inspector in any part of Unity.

Now we need to call the `DrawInspectedItemGUI` function from the method `OnInspectorGUI` of the `LevelInspector` class:

```
public override void OnInspectorGUI () {
  // DrawDefaultInspector();
  DrawLevelDataGUI ();
  DrawLevelSizeGUI ();
  DrawPieceSelectedGUI ();
  DrawInspectedItemGUI ();
  if (GUI.changed) {
    EditorUtility.SetDirty (_myTarget);
  }
}
```

Finally, update the `ModeHandler` method in order to repaint the inspector every time we change the mode in the Level Creator tool:

```
private void ModeHandler () {
  switch (_selectedMode) {
  case Mode.Paint:
  case Mode.Edit:
  case Mode.Erase:
    Tools.current = Tool.None;
    break;
  case Mode.View:
  default:
    Tools.current = Tool.View;
    break;
  }

  if(_selectedMode != _currentMode) {
    _currentMode = _selectedMode;
    _itemInspected = null;
    Repaint();
  }
  // Force 2D Mode!
  SceneView.currentDrawingSceneView.in2DMode = true;
}
```

To test this, save the changes and wait for Unity to compile, then repeat the process you did for testing the `Paint` method but now add at least one Sign.

Now, select the **Edit** mode and click on the Sign level piece prefab. You will see this on the bottom of the Level Inspector:

The sign piece inspector is being rendered inside the Level Inspector; now, with one click you have access to the custom options for the piece.

Using the Handles class

In this section, we are going to extend the capabilities to the Edit mode, allowing the user to also reallocate the position of the pieces in the grid. To achieve this, we will use the class Handles.

In Unity, a handle is a 3D control you use to manipulate items in the Scene View. The Handles class allows you to use several built-in handle GUIs, such as the tools to position, scale, and rotate an object via the Transform component. Let's take a look at the following screenshot:

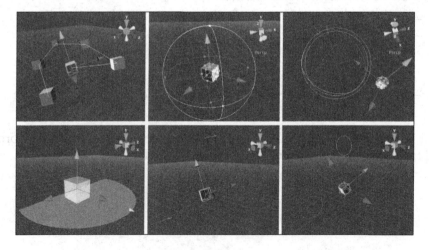

The `Handles` class is also used to add the GUI to the Scene View. We did that at the beginning of the chapter using the methods `BeginGUI` and `EndGUI`.

Let's make the necessary changes to make this work. Let's add this code snippet defining two variables to the `LevelInspector` class to save the original position of the piece:

```
private int _originalPosX;
private int _originalPosY;
```

Then we will create a new method called `Move`:

```
private void Move() {
  Vector3 gridPoint =
  _myTarget.WorldToGridCoordinates
  (_itemInspected.transform.position);
  int col = (int) gridPoint.x;
  int row = (int) gridPoint.y;

  if(col == _originalPosX && row == _originalPosY) {
    return;
  }

  if(!_myTarget.IsInsideGridBounds(col,row) ||
  _myTarget.Pieces[col + row * _myTarget.TotalColumns] != null) {
    _itemInspected.transform.position =
    _myTarget.GridToWorldCoordinates( _originalPosX,
    _originalPosY);
  } else {
    _myTarget.Pieces[ _originalPosX + _originalPosY *
    _myTarget.TotalColumns] = null;
    _myTarget.Pieces[col + row * _myTarget.TotalColumns] =
    _itemInspected.GetComponent<LevelPiece>();
    _myTarget.Pieces[col + row *
    _myTarget.TotalColumns].transform.position =
    _myTarget.GridToWorldCoordinates(col,row);
  }
}
```

This method will check whether the final position of the piece is different from the original one, and if it is, it will check whether the new position is empty. If the movement is not possible, the piece is returned to the original position.

It's time to add a handle. We are going to update the method `EventHandler`. Inside the switch statement, replace the content of the Edit case with this:

```
case Mode.Edit:
  if(Event.current.type == EventType.MouseDown) {
    Edit(col , row);
    _originalPosX = col;
    _originalPosY = row;
  }
  if(Event.current.type == EventType.MouseUp ||
     Event.current.type == EventType.Ignore) {
    if(_itemInspected != null) {
      Move ();
    }
  }

  if(_itemInspected != null) {
    _itemInspected.transform.position =
      Handles.FreeMoveHandle(
        _itemInspected.transform.position,
        _itemInspected.transform.rotation,
        Level.GridSize / 2 ,
        Level.GridSize / 2 * Vector3.one,
        Handles.RectangleCap);
  }
  break;
```

Now when Edit mode is activated, if the user makes a click we will proceed as usual but will also save the position of that click (the original position of a piece if there is a piece there).

If the user releases the mouse button during the movement, the method `Move` will perform the logic to reallocate the piece in the level. We added the event `Ignore` to capture the situation of the mouse outside the Scene View.

To perform the movement, all the work is delegated to the handle. We used the method `FreeMoveHandle` to do this. This method receives as parameters the position, rotation, size of the handle (in this case, the grid size), a vector with the size to snap, and a method to use for drawing the handle. The result will be a square around the piece and the new position.

Save the changes and wait for Unity to compile, create a new level, and paint several pieces on it; then, click on **Edit** and start moving these pieces. Let's take a look at the following screenshot:

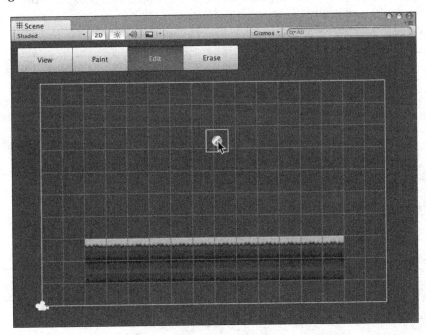

The `Handle` class is a very useful class for manipulating content in the Scene View. To learn more about it, visit `http://docs.unity3d.com/ScriptReference/Handles.html`.

Adding the final details to Level Creator

The Level Creator is almost ready, but before finishing this chapter, let's make a few improvements to make this tool better.

Using hiding flags

Currently, each time we paint pieces on the level, they are created and nested in the level game object. We are still able to access the objects directly; this means it is possible to move a piece by error outside the grid. Let's take a look at the following screenshot:

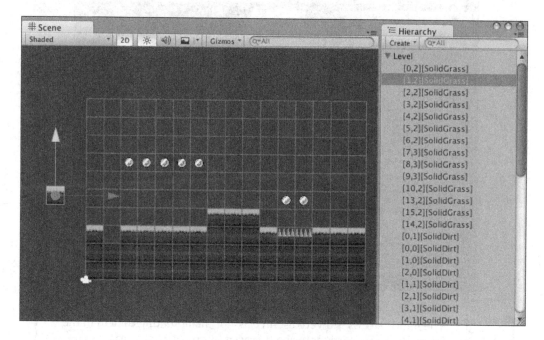

To control the visibility of the level pieces in the hierarchy, we are going to use `HidingFlags`, bit masks that control object destruction, saving, and visibility in inspectors. Here is a list of available flags that could be applied to Unity objects:

- `None`: A normal and visible object. This is the default.
- `HideInHierarchy`: It does not appear in the hierarchy.

- `HideInInspector`: It is not visible in the inspector.

- `DontSaveInEditor`: It is not saved to the scene in the editor.

- `NotEditable`: It is not editable in the inspector.

- `DontUnloadUnusedAsset`: It is not unloaded by `Resources.UnloadUnusedAssets`.

- `DontSaveInBuild`: It is not saved when a player is built.

- `DontSave`: It is not saved to the scene. It will not be destroyed when a new scene is loaded. It is a shortcut for **HideFlags.DontSaveInBuild | HideFlags.DontSaveInEditor | HideFlags.DontUnloadUnusedAsset**.

- `HideAndDontSave`: It is a combination of not shown in the hierarchy, not saved to scenes, and not unloaded by the object; it will not be unloaded by `Resources.UnloadUnusedAssets`.

In our case, the flag we want to use is `HideInHierarchy`. To use it, we will update the `Paint` method as follows:

```
private void Paint(int col, int row) {
    // Check out of bounds and if we have a piece selected
    if(!_myTarget.IsInsideGridBounds(col,row) || _pieceSelected ==
    null) {
        return;
    }
    // Check if I need to destroy a previous piece
    if(_myTarget.Pieces[col + row * _myTarget.TotalColumns] != null)
    {
        DestroyImmediate(_myTarget.Pieces[col + row *
        _myTarget.TotalColumns].gameObject);
    }
    // Do paint !
    GameObject obj = PrefabUtility.InstantiatePrefab(
    _pieceSelected.gameObject) as GameObject;
    obj.transform.parent = _myTarget.transform;
    obj.name = string.Format("[{0},{1}] [{2}]", col, row, obj.name);
    obj.transform.position = _myTarget.GridToWorldCoordinates(col,
    row);
    obj.hideFlags = HideFlags.HideInHierarchy;
    _myTarget.Pieces[col + row * _myTarget.TotalColumns] =
    obj.GetComponent<LevelPiece>();
}
```

Each time we generate a new prefab instance of a level piece, we will set up the `HidingFlags` to `HideInHierarchy`.

Save the changes and wait for Unity to compile; then, create a new level and start painting pieces on the grid. Take a look at the hierarchy; it doesn't matter how many pieces we added to the level. These are not accessible unless we use the Level Creator modes to interact with them. Take a look at the following screenshot:

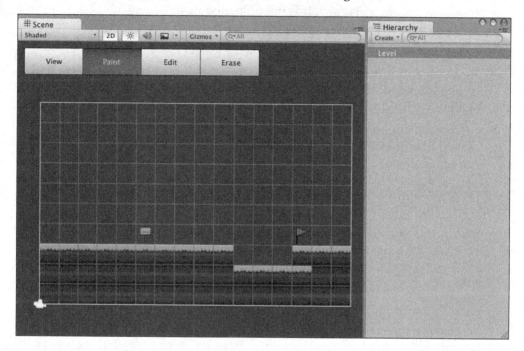

With this improvement, we are making users follow the workflow of the Level Creator tool and avoiding possible corruption of the level.

Finally, one of the important restrictions to make Level Creator work is to avoid making changes in its transform property.

It's hard to assume the users of the Level Creator tool are going to keep this without making changes. So, instead of giving them this responsibility, we are going to implement this restriction through code using a hiding Flag.

Add the following line of code inside the InitLevel method:

```
_myTarget.transform.hideFlags = HideFlags.NotEditable;
```

Save and check the inspector of the **Level**:

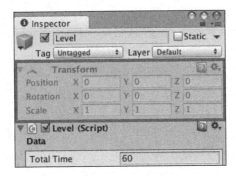

Summary

In this chapter, we learned about how to add a GUI to the Scene View and change its common behavior.

The Scene View is an editor window that allows you to preview and interact with your scene. You can add a custom GUI using the methods BeginGUI and EndGUI from the Handles class.

The Handles class is also useful to help us to manipulate game objects in the scene, creating specific GUI that allows modification of the transform of these objects.

We also learned to use the HidingFlags, allowing us to manipulate the visibility of our game objects in the Editor and also to control whether they are going to be saved to disk or not. This becomes handy when you need extra control to make your custom tools.

You can capture events in the Scene View using the Event class, and can use that input to trigger your custom methods.

We now have all the GUI and workflow implemented for our Level Creator. In the next chapter, we will pay attention to the look and feel of our tool.

6

Changing the Look and Feel of the Editor with GUI Styles and GUI Skins

When we talk about the look and feel of a GUI, we refer to how colors, shapes, layout, and typefaces are used in an application, which is the "look", and how buttons, menus, and other components behave in the application, which is the "feel".

Defining a good look and feel will help an application to have its own character, make a good first impression, and in some cases improve its usability.

In Unity we can modify how our editor GUI components look, and in certain cases we can even modify how they behave using the classes GUIStyle and GUISkin in our custom tools.

Here, you will learn how to modify the look of the editor GUI and how to apply this in the Level Creator tool.

In this chapter, we will cover the following topics:

- Creating and using instances of the class GUIStyle
- Creating and using instances of the class GUISkin
- Understanding the difference between GUIStyle and GUISkin

Overview

The GUIStyle and GUISkin classes allow us to modify the look and feel of our GUI components.

These classes were originally used to customize the GUI of a video game developed in previous versions of Unity. After 4.6, and with the inclusion of a better UI system, their use refocused to helping with the customization of the Editor GUI. These two classes give the developers enough flexibility to make their tools look "professional" and have their own identity.

Defining the chapter goals

In this chapter, we will use the GUIStyle and GUISkin classes to modify the look and feel of the Level Creator tool.

The goals here are:

- Modifying the look and feel of the Level custom inspector to make clear the different sections it has
- Modifying the look and feel of the Palette window to make the top buttons (toolbar) look more like tabs

The final result will look like this:

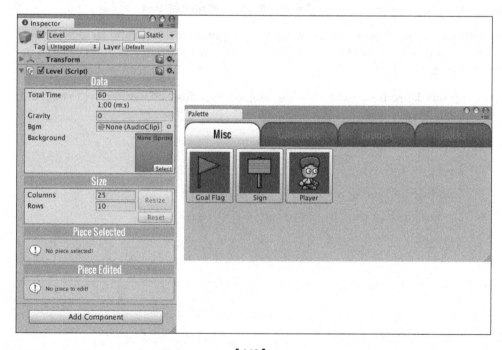

Changing the look and feel of the Level Creator tool

In this section, we will modify the current look and feel of our tool.

Using GUIStyles in our GUI components

The GUIStyle class is part of the UnityEditor namespace, and is used to define the style of a single GUI control, such as a button, a label, or a text area. Most of the methods used to create these GUI components accept an optional GUIStyle parameter to override their default style.

Let's check the current look of the level inspector:

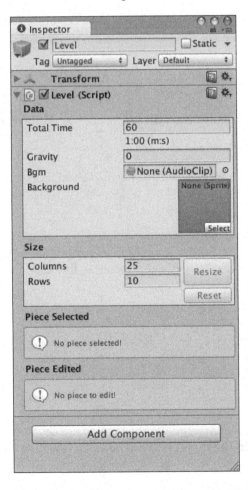

We divided the inspector into four sections, and each one has a title. In the previous chapters, we used something like this to make the text of these labels look different:

```
EditorGUILayout.LabelField("MyTitle", EditorStyles.boldLabel);
```

We made all the title texts look bold using the class EditorStyles.

The class EditorStyles contain these GUIStyle instances commonly used by Unity to style their GUI components. Here, we have a huge number of styles available that respect the native Unity look and feel.

> If you want to check more about the EditorStyles class, visit: http://docs.unity3d.com/ScriptReference/EditorStyles.html.

The titles are OK but we want to make something better, so we will create our own custom GUIStyle instance.

Let's add a new member variable inside the LevelInspector class:

```
private GUIStyle _titleStyle;
```

Then, let's create a new method called InitStyles and copy the following code:

```
private void InitStyles() {
    _titleStyle = new GUIStyle();
    _titleStyle.alignment = TextAnchor.MiddleCenter;
    _titleStyle.fontSize = 16;
}
```

Here, we created a new GUIStyle instance called _titleStyle and defined its alignment and font size. With that done, the only thing we need to do is call the InitStyles method inside the method OnEnable, like this:

```
private void OnEnable () {
    //Debug.Log ("OnEnable was called...");
    _myTarget = (Level)target;
    InitLevel ();
    ResetResizeValues ();
    SubscribeEvents();
    InitStyles();
}
```

Now, replace all the EditorStyles.boldLabel instances with the _titleStyle variable. For example, in the method DrawLevelDataGUI, you will find something like this:

```
EditorGUILayout.LabelField ("Data", EditorStyles.boldLabel);
```

The idea is to update the line to something like this:

```
EditorGUILayout.LabelField ("Data", _titleStyle);
```

If you check the Level custom inspector, you will notice the change in the title's look and feel:

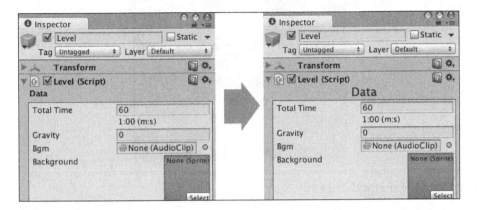

When you work with the GUIStyle instances, you will also use resources such as textures and fonts to improve the look and feel of your GUI components. To learn how to do this, grab the **Color_Bg.png** and **Oswald-Regular.ttf** files from the book content and add them to a folder called **Resources** inside Tools/LevelCreator/Editor:

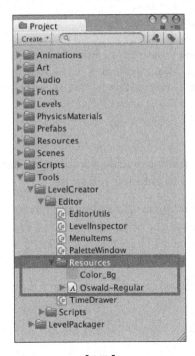

Remember, every time you want to use a texture in an editor GUI context, you must change the attribute **Texture Type** to **Editor GUI and Legacy GUI** on the inspector associated to it:

Let's update the method `InitStyles`:

```
private void InitStyles() {
    _titleStyle = new GUIStyle();
    _titleStyle.alignment = TextAnchor.MiddleCenter;
    _titleStyle.fontSize = 16;

Texture2D titleBg = (Texture2D)
        Resources.Load("Color_Bg");
        Font titleFont = (Font)
        Resources.Load("Oswald-Regular");
    _titleStyle.normal.background = titleBg;
    _titleStyle.normal.textColor = Color.white;
    _titleStyle.font = titleFont;


}
```

Because the texture and the font are inside a folder called `Resources`, we can just use the `Resources.Load` method to get their reference.

We assign the texture as a background for the label; to have access to this property, we write `_titleStyle.normal.background = titleBg`.

In this case, normal is a GUIStyleState, a class that has specialized values for a given state. These values are the background and text color.

There are several GUIStyleState class types, but we will talk more about these later. Because the GUI component for which we are trying to modify the look and feel is a label, the only valid one is normal.

Save and check the changes. Now, the different sections in this inspector are clearly defined:

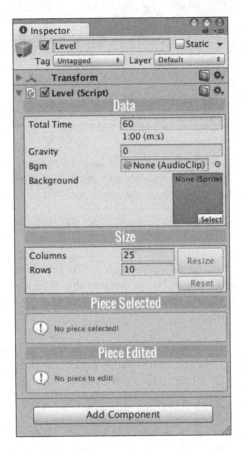

Now, you have the idea about how to work with the GUIStyle class. In the next section, we will continue modifying the look and feel of the Level Creator tool focusing on the Palette window.

Working with the GUIStyleState instances

Before coding, let's take a look at how the Palette window looks:

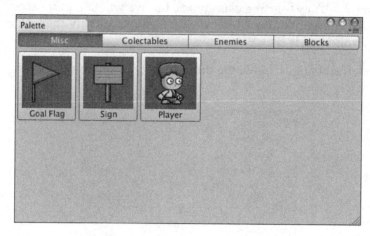

The current GUI is ok, but there is a room for improvement. The original idea for the Palette window was to map categories to tabs. When the user selects a tab, the content associated to that category is displayed.

Here we will make the top buttons, created using the `GUILayout.Toolbar` method, look like tabs.

For each tab, we will have three different states. The first state is normal, where the tab is not selected. The next state is hover, where the cursor is over the tab. The last state is selected, where the tab is selected; this means the category associated to this tab is displayed in the scrollable area.

For each state, we will need a texture. So, grab from the book contents the `Tab_Normal.png` and `Tab_Selected.png` files and copy them inside of the `Tools\LevelCreator\Editor\Resources` folder.

The following image shows the different textures:

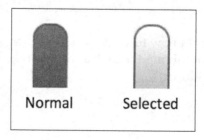

Now, we will repeat the process we did for the labels in the level inspector class, but for the Palette window. In the `PaletteWindow` class, add a new member variable:

```
private GUIStyle _tabStyle;
```

Then create a new method called `InitStyles` and copy the following code:

```
private void InitStyles() {

    _tabStyle = new GUIStyle();
    _tabStyle.alignment = TextAnchor.MiddleCenter;
    _tabStyle.fontSize = 16;

}
```

Add this method at the end of the `OnEnable` method. Until this point it is similar to what we did with the Level custom inspector.

To work with the different states that the buttons on the toolbar can have, we will make use of the `GUIStyleState` instances inside the `GUIStyle`. The following list contains the available ones:

- `normal`: This renders settings for when the component is displayed normally
- `hover`: This renders settings for when the mouse hovers over the control
- `active`: This renders settings for when the control is pressed down
- `onNormal`: This renders settings for when the control is turned on
- `onHover`: This renders settings for when the control is turned on and the mouse hovers over it
- `onActive`: This renders settings for when the element is turned on and pressed down
- `focused`: This renders settings for when the element has a keyboard focus
- `onFocused`: This renders settings for when the element has a keyboard focus and is turned on

In this case, the normal state of a tab will be represented by the normal `GUIStyleState`, and the selected state will be represented by a combination of `onNormal` and `onFocused` `GUIStyleState` instances.

Let's update the InitStyles method:

```
private void InitStyles() {

    _tabStyle = new GUIStyle();
    _tabStyle.alignment = TextAnchor.MiddleCenter;
    _tabStyle.fontSize = 16;

        Texture2D tabNormal = (Texture2D)
      Resources.Load("Tab_Normal");
    Texture2D tabSelected = (Texture2D)
      Resources.Load("Tab_Selected");
    Font tabFont = (Font) Resources.Load("Oswald-Regular");
    _tabStyle.font = tabFont;
    _tabStyle.fixedHeight = 40;
    _tabStyle.normal.background = tabNormal;
    _tabStyle.normal.textColor = Color.grey;

    _tabStyle.onNormal.background = tabSelected;
    _tabStyle.onNormal.textColor = Color.black;

    _tabStyle.onFocused.background = tabSelected;
    _tabStyle.onFocused.textColor = Color.black;
}
```

Now it is time to update the method in charge of rendering the toolbar in order to use the new GUIStyle method we created. Update the method DrawTabs to look like this:

```
private void DrawTabs () {
        int index = (int)_categorySelected;
        EditorGUILayout.Space();
        index = GUILayout.Toolbar (index, _categoryLabels.ToArray
        (), _tabStyle);
        _categorySelected = _categories [index];
    }
```

Save and wait for Unity to compile the changes. Then, open the Palette window; you will see something like this:

Now the buttons look more like tabs, however, the texture of the tabs is not displayed properly because it is stretched. This is because Unity stretches the texture to fill the area occupied by the GUI component by default. To solve this problem, we need to add an extra line of code at the end of the InitStyles method:

```
_tabStyle.border = new RectOffset(18, 18, 20, 4);
```

With this, we defined a border for the textures that we are using for the tabs, this means all the content that corresponds to the margins (left, right, top, and bottom, respectively) won't be stretched, only the center will be.

Now, if you take a look again to the Palette window, you will see that the textures used for the tabs look good:

Changing the look and feel using a simpler approach

In this section, we will cover a new approach to customizing the look and feel of our custom tools using the GUISkin asset.

Creating a GUISkin asset

The way we modified the look and feel of the Level Creator tool wasn't complicated, but it requires time and a considerable effort in terms of making modifications in the code and seeing the results we expect. The good news is that there is an alternative approach to achieving the same result using the GUISkin assets.

In Unity, a GUISkin asset is a collection of the GUIStyle instances that can be used in our custom GUI, and it is intended to allow you to apply style to an entire GUI instead of a single component by itself.

The GUISkin class is part of the UnityEngine namespace and extends from the ScriptableObject class. We are going to talk more about Scriptable Objects in *Chapter 7, Saving Data in a Persistent Way with Scriptable Objects.*

Because of the nature of the GUISkin, which required to be created as an asset, you can create a specific kind of look and feel and reuse it across several projects. If you had experience working with web development, you can imagine a GUISkin asset to be like a css file.

Let's create a new GUISkin. Go to the project browser and navigate to **Tools | LevelCreator | Editor | Resources**, then navigate to **Create | GUI Skin**, as shown in the following screenshot:

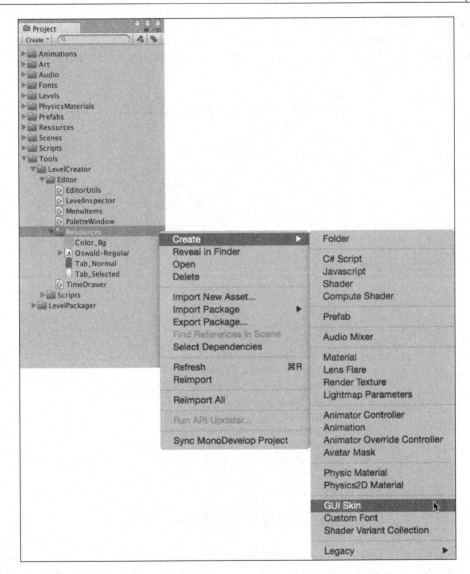

This creates a GUISkin asset in the folder **Resources**. Change the name of this asset to **LevelCreatorSkin**.

If you select the **LevelCreatorSkin** asset, you will notice that it generates its own inspector. This means that it is easier to modify the values of the GUISkin asset because you don't need to deal with different attributes using code, as shown in the following screenshot:

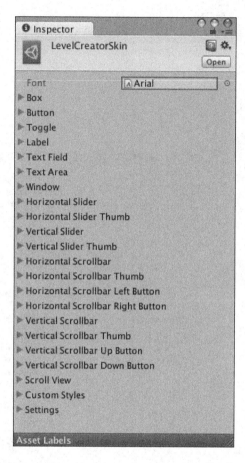

In the preceding image, you can see that there is a GUIStyle property for all the GUI components we used. For example, if you expand the property with the name **Label**, you will see most of the properties that we modified at the beginning of the chapter to customize the titles of the level inspector:

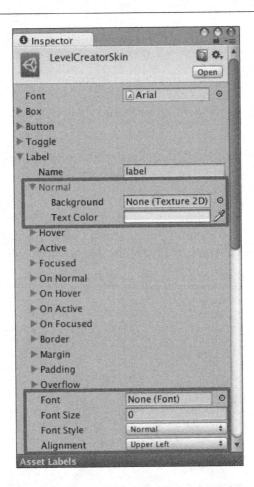

To give a shoot to this approach, we will refactor the code we created in the
LevelInspector class.

Integrating and using a GUISkin

Go to the class LevelInspector and update the method InitStyles to match the
following:

```
private void InitStyles() {
        GUISkin skin = (GUISkin) Resources.
Load("LevelCreatorSkin");
        _titleStyle = skin.label;
    }
```

[Remember to check whether you have your `GUISkin` asset in a `Resources` folder!]

Here, we load the `LevelCreatorSkin` asset and then assign the `GUIStyle` label to the `_titleStyle` variable.

If you check the custom inspector of the level class, you will notice that all the changes we made at the beginning have disappeared (well, we removed almost all the code, what did you expect?).

Don't worry; we will fix everything in less than a minute. Select the **LevelCreatorSkin** asset and expand the property **Label**. Then, assign the font **Oswald-Regular** and set the size to **16** and the alignment to **Middle Center**:

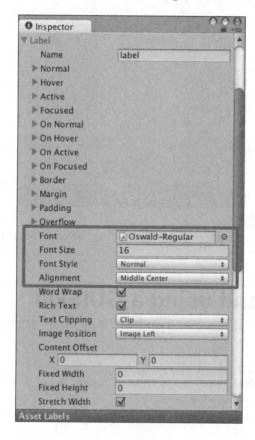

Finally, go to the property **Normal** and assign the texture **Color_Bg** to **Background** and a white color to **Text Color**:

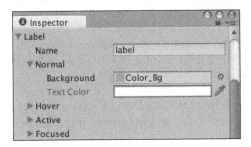

Now, save and that's it! You just achieved the same result that we did at the beginning in the inspector using less code and less time. As an exercise, try to do the same with the Palette window:

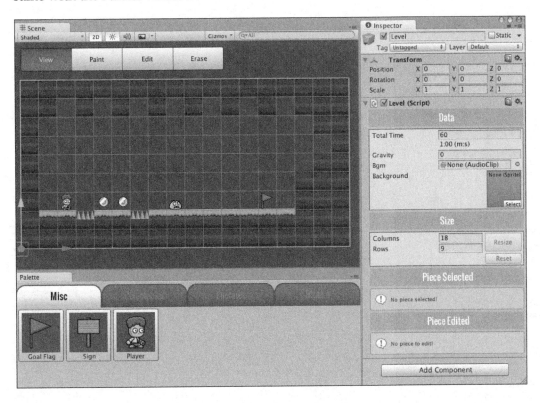

The good thing about this approach is that because the GUISkin asset exposes all the properties, it is easier to discover and test new configurations in terms of look and feel.

Summary

In this chapter, you learned how to customize the look and feel of our custom tools using GUIStyle and GUISkin instances.

For a specific item, it is good to use a GUIStyle instance to modify how a GUI component is rendered, but if you want something more scalable and less tight to your code, a GUISkin will be a better option.

With this chapter, we have finished our Level Creator Tool and now we are ready to move to other challenges related to improving the development workflow of *Run & Jump*.

In the next chapter, we are going to explore the use of Scriptable Objects.

7

Saving Data in a Persistent Way with Scriptable Objects

When you are in the final stage of the implementation of features for your video game, the next step is usually polishing and tweaking, investing most of the time to finding those special values that make your video game awesome and unique.

It is annoying when you find those values in your video game and suddenly you realize you were in Play mode. At this point, you have two options; you can either write down all these values, sometimes they are a lot, or start over.

In Unity, there is a special type of class called **Scriptable Object**, which is mainly used as a data container. One of its characteristics, if is used correctly, is the ability to save the changes you make to the scene during the Play mode.

You will learn how to create and use Scriptable Objects in Unity and use them to contain gameplay parameters from a level in *Run & Jump*.

The main topics that will be covered in this chapter are:

- Creating the Scriptable Object
- Saving and consuming data from a Scriptable Object

Overview

A Scriptable Object is a Unity special object type that doesn't need to be attached to a game object on a scene to exist, because it can be saved as an asset in the project. This class is used as a base for most of the special editor classes that we saw in the previous chapters, such as the `Editor` and `EditorWindow` class. However, the principal use for that in this chapter is to going to be saving data in a persistent way.

In some scenarios, this has benefits over using XML, JSON, or plain text files because Unity will handle all the serializing and parsing for you without the necessity of a custom parser or third-party tool.

When you create tools for game designers, you may want to allow them to experiment with values that affect how the video game behaves.

In this chapter, you will learn how to use Scriptable Objects to store data and make it persist in the Play mode.

Defining the chapter goals

In this chapter, we will use Scriptable Objects to allow game designers to tweak level settings in real time. In this case, we will focus on the gravity of the level but the bgm and background of the level will also be included to make this implementation complete.

The goal here are:

- Implementing a level settings class using Scriptable Objects
- Creating an asset based on the level settings class
- Integrating the Scriptable Object to the Level class

Preparing the environment

Before we start playing with Scriptable Objects, we are going to play with the gravity of a custom level an see what happens.

Updatable gravity in levels

Right now, if you want to adjust the gravity of a level you must to make the changes before pressing the Play button in order to see results.

The Level class has a method called SetGravity, which is responsible for taking the value of the gravity property and applying it to the **Physics 2D** settings in Unity. You don't need to take care about how this is implemented. The only thing we must to do is to integrate this in the custom inspector we created for the Level class, so each time the gravity value changes, the SetGravity method will take care of the rest.

Let's update the `LevelInspector` class to achieve this. At the end of the `DrawLevelDataGUI` method, add the following line of code:

```
_myTarget.SetGravity();
```

This method checks the value of the gravity and updates this if necessary. Pretty simple!

Playing with gravity

Using the Level Creator tool, we will try to replicate the following level:

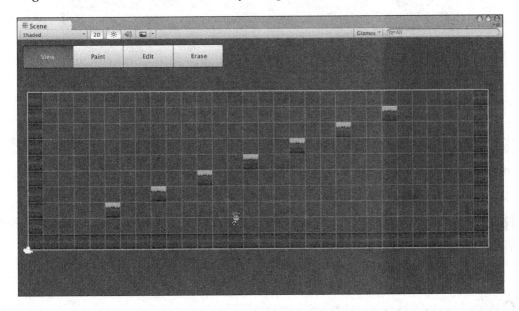

We will use this level for testing purposes in this chapter, so save the scene inside the `Levels` folder with the name `Test_level`.

Press the **Play** button and start playing the level. If you decrease the gravity value, Timmy, the player character, will be able to jump higher. If you increase the gravity value, the opposite will happen.

Adjust the gravity until you can jump the central platform with a single jump, and then exit the play mode:

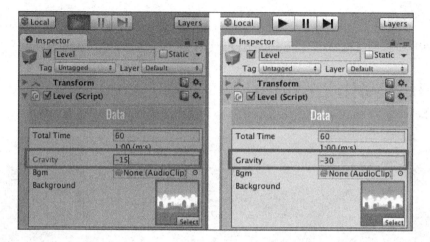

After exiting the play mode, the gravity returns to the original value. In video games where a lot of variables need to be tweaked and tested, the ability of keeping the changes of play mode allows the game designers to go across this task quickly.

Implementing a Scriptable Object

In this section, we will create a ScriptableObject class and then reallocate the gravity, bgm, and background variables there.

Creating the data class

The ScriptableObject class is part of the UnityEngine namespace. You derive from this class if you want to create objects that don't need to be attached to a game object, but more often, if you are looking for objects meant to save data.

Let's create a script called LevelSettings.cs inside the folder Scripts/Levels and add the following code:

```
using UnityEngine;
using System;

namespace RunAndJump {

  [Serializable]
  public class LevelSettings : ScriptableObject {

    public float gravity = -30;
```

```
    public AudioClip bgm;
    public Sprite background;
  }
}
```

The first step was to make the class extend from the ScriptableObject class. Then, we added the public variables to represent each variable we want to save in this class.

We added the namespace System to use the attribute Serializable. Using this attribute, we tell Unity to serialize all the public properties of the class. This is very important in order to make them persist!

 If you want to know more about the scriptable objects, visit: http://docs.unity3d.com/ScriptReference/ScriptableObject.html.

Generating an asset to contain the data class

All the instance of a scriptable object are saved in Unity as assets; this means you can reference this asset in any script you want, in the same way you use materials, for example.

To generate these instances, we will create a method in the EditorUtils class called CreateAsset:

```
public static T CreateAsset<T>(string path)
    where T : ScriptableObject {
    T dataClass = (T) ScriptableObject.CreateInstance<T>();
    AssetDatabase.CreateAsset(dataClass, path);
    AssetDatabase.Refresh();
    AssetDatabase.SaveAssets();
    return dataClass;
}
```

This method receives a generic type, which must to be a Scriptable Object, and a path. With those values, the method will create an asset in the specified path using the T class.

The CreateAsset method uses the AssetDatabase class apart from the UnityEditor namespace. The method CreateAsset does the main part, then the Refresh method makes the new asset visible in the project, and finally, the SaveAssets method saves the new created asset in the project.

Now, it is time to make this method available in Unity, so let's create a new menu item by adding a new method in the class `MenuItems`:

```
[MenuItem ("Tools/Level Creator/New Level Settings")]
    private static void NewLevelSettings () {
        string path = EditorUtility.SaveFilePanelInProject(
            "New Level Settings",
            "LevelSettings",
            "asset",
            "Define the name for the LevelSettings asset");
        if(path != "") {
            EditorUtils.CreateAsset<LevelSettings>(path);
        }
    }
```

Before using the method we created in the `EditorUtils` class, we call the `SaveFilePanelInProject` method from the `EditorUtility` class. This will show a window asking for the name and location for the asset we want to create.

Using the path returned by the `SaveFilePanelInProject` method, we proceed to create the asset.

We add an `If` statement to check whether the path is different from an empty string; this happens if the user clicks on **Cancel** on the window created by the `SaveFilePanelInProject` method.

Save and wait for Unity to compile. Then, go to the Unity menu and navigate to **Tools | Level Creator | New Level Settings**:

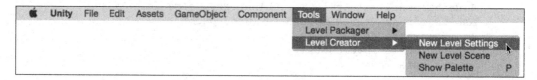

Now, you will see the **Save File** dialog. Create a new folder called **LevelSettings** in the root of the project. Inside this, create a new asset called **Normal.asset**, as shown in the following screenshot:

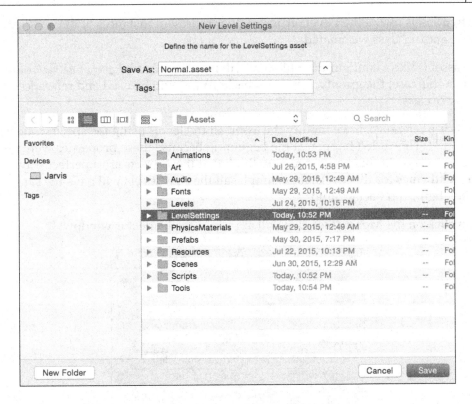

Repeat the process and create an extra asset called **Moon.asset**. Your project browser will look as follows:

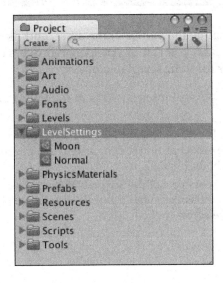

The two assets inside the **LevelSettings** folder represent instances of the
LevelSetting class we created.

Each asset is like a configuration file that will be referenced by a MonoBehaviour
class. In this case, the gravity, bgm, and background will be used and referenced by
the Level class.

As this is a reference, if we modify the asset, all the levels using the specific one will
be affected. This didn't happen at the beginning because these properties were inside
the Level class. At this point, you may think that these assets are a perfect way
to create themes for the levels, for example, all the easy levels will have the same
gravity, bgm, and backgrounds.

If you click on the **Moon** asset, this will appear in the inspector window:

Here, you can directly change the values of the asset, and like the usual inspectors
for our MonoBehaviour class, you can use property drawers or decorator drawers, or
create a custom inspector for your scriptable object.

In the rest of the chapter, we will integrate this to the levels in *Run & Jump*.

> If you remember the chapter about custom inspectors and editor
> windows, we talked about the OnEnable, OnDisable and OnDestroy
> message methods.
>
> These methods are part of the ScriptableObject class. The Editor and
> EditorWindow classes extend from the ScriptableObject class and that is
> why you have access to them.

Integrating the Scriptable Object with the level

In this section, we will integrate the `LevelSetting` class with our levels and then test how Scriptable Objects allow us to modify values in the play mode.

Updating the Level and the LevelInspector class

The first change to be made is to update the `Level` class. So, instead of using the current variables for the gravity, bgm, and background, start using a `LevelSetting` class as a reference.

Let's make a small update in `Level.cs` file. Add the following lines to it:

```
[SerializeField]
  private LevelSettings _settings;

  public LevelSettings Settings {
    get { return _settings; }
    set { _settings = value; }
  }
```

We need to take care of the render of this new property.

We will update the `DrawLevelDataGUI` method in the `LevelInspector` class:

```
private void DrawLevelDataGUI () {
    EditorGUILayout.LabelField ("Data", _titleStyle);
    EditorGUILayout.BeginVertical ("box");
    EditorGUILayout.PropertyField (_serializedTotalTime);
    _myTarget.Settings = (LevelSettings) EditorGUILayout.
    ObjectField("Level Settings", _myTarget.Settings,
    typeof(LevelSettings), false);
    if(_myTarget.Settings != null) {
      Editor.CreateEditor(_myTarget.Settings).OnInspectorGUI();
    } else {
      EditorGUILayout.HelpBox("You must attach a LevelSettings
      asset!", MessageType.Warning);
    }
    EditorGUILayout.EndVertical ();
    _myTarget.SetGravity();
  }
```

We removed all the lines related to rendering the GUI for the gravity, bgm, and background fields and used the same approach that we used in *Chapter 5, Customizing the Scene View*, to render the inspector of the LevelSettings Scriptable Object.

Now, back in the Level class, we will modify the C# properties of the gravity, bgm, and background variables in order to use the LevelSettings instance:

```
public float Gravity {
        get { return ((_settings != null) ? _settings.gravity : 0); }
        set {
          if(_settings != null) {
            _settings.gravity = value;
          }
        }
}


    public AudioClip Bgm {
      get { return (_settings != null) ? _settings.bgm : null; }
      set {
        if(_settings != null) {
          _settings.bgm = value;
            }
          }
    }


    public Sprite Background {
      get { return (_settings != null) ? _settings.background : null;
}
      set {
        if(_settings != null) {
          _settings.background = value;
            }
          }
    }
```

Finally, comment the following lines of code (we don't need these anymore):

```
// [SerializeField]
// private float _gravity = -30;
// [SerializeField]
// private AudioClip _bgm;
// [SerializeField]
// private Sprite _background;
```

These updates will keep the change we did transparent for the rest of the *Run & Jump* implementation.

Save and wait for Unity to compile. Then, select a level scene; you will see a new field in the level custom inspector:

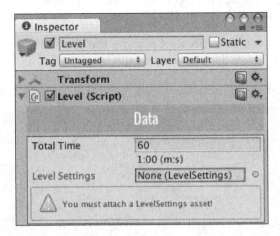

Now, drag **Moon.asset** to the **Settings** field. As soon this is done, you will see the **Gravity** field appear in the custom inspector with the **Bgm** and **Background** fields:

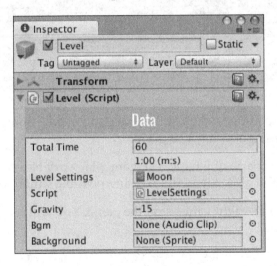

Perfect! Now that we have successfully integrated the scriptable object in our level, it is time to start tweaking the gravity!

Tweaking the level settings in the play mode

Open the level we created at the beginning, **Test_level**, and attach the **Moon** asset to the **Settings** field. Now, click on the **Play** button.

If you select the **View** tab, you can start playing the game. Press the spacebar to jump and use the arrows to move Timmy around the level:

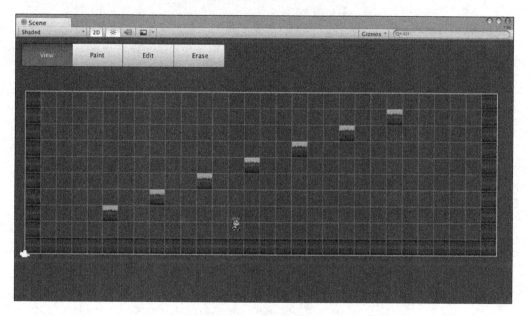

This level has seven platforms. Adjust the gravity to make Timmy reach the first four platforms from left to right using a single jump.

This is a simplified scenario of what tweak gameplay variables can be, but you should get the idea and also extend this to other possible situations.

As soon as you reach the right value, stop the game. You will see that the new gravity value remains.

Now, based on the level settings you use, your level can be easy, hard, or impossible to beat, and by that I mean you will not be able to finish the level. The good thing is, you have the basic tools to make the necessary tweaks to avoid impossible levels.

Summary

Scriptable Objects are not the most used feature of Unity but are useful it is good to keep them in the solution sets approaches for our video game.

They are used as assets, which are only meant to store data, but can also be used to help serialize objects and can be instantiated in our scenes. In some scenarios, they are also an alternative to XML, JSON, or plain text files to define configuration parameters.

Based on what we did in this chapter, with a Scriptable Object approach, it is now possible to keep changes you make to settings values while your game is running in play mode, easily swap between different sets of settings values, and allowing the separation of logic and data.

In the next chapter, we are going to work improving the asset import pipeline.

8

Controlling the Import Pipeline Using AssetPostprocessor Scripts

If you have a growing video game project and your artists or other team members constantly drop assets in Unity, there is no doubt you have experienced the problem of having to manage the import settings on all of those assets.

Most of the time, importing assets is subject to errors, as somebody in the team often forgets to set the right parameters for them. Due to these kind of situations, automating the import pipeline of our video game project is important.

Fortunately, Unity has a feature called AssetPostprocessor, which allows us to hook actions prior to or after importing an asset.

You will learn how to get your own AssetPostprocessor classes up and running to customize and integrate assets directly into the *Run & Jump* video game project.

In this chapter, we will cover the following topics:

- Using the AssetPostprocessor API
- DLL creation

Overview

The **AssetPostprocessor** is a class meant to help us to automate the process of applying specific configurations to the assets imported.

Is up to you how you define the criteria for applying or not a specific configuration, for example you can use a system based on the location of the imported asset or detecting keywords in the asset name to do several things such as adding scripts to objects, adding colliders to objects, or changing settings to textures.

In order to guarantee the availability of the `AssetPostprocessor` scripts you are going to implement, it is good practice to use a **DLL** to group them and use the DLL inside the `Editor` folder in your target video game project. If you don't use a DLL and something in the project fails to compile, your assets are not going to be configured as you was planned.

Defining the chapter goals

In this chapter, we will create a DLL using the `AssetPostprocessor` class to control the import pipeline of the background and level pieces images in *Run & Jump*.

The goals here are:

- Implementing the `AssetPostprocessor` class to format images
- Creating a new DLL with the `AssetPostprocessor` classes inside it and integrating the DLL with Run & Jump.

Using the AssetPostprocessor class

The `AssetPostprocessor` class is part of the `UnityEditor` namespace, and must be extended for any class intended to control the asset import pipeline. This class has several message methods to react when an asset is imported.

To start with, we will create a folder in the *Run & Jump* project called `ImportPipeline`. Place this folder inside the `Tools` folder.

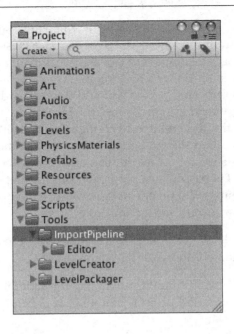

Inside the ImportPipeline folder add an Editor folder and then create a script
called TexturePipeline.cs. Add the following code:

```
using UnityEngine;
using UnityEditor;
namespace RunAndJump.ImportPipeline {
  public class TexturePipeline : AssetPostprocessor {

    private void OnPreprocessTexture () {
      Debug.LogFormat("OnPreprocessTexture, The path is {0}",
      assetPath);
    }

    private void OnPostprocessTexture (Texture2D texture) {
      Debug.LogFormat("OnPostprocessTexture, The path is {0}",
      assetPath);
    }
  }
}
```

Since the `TexturePipeline` class needs to know when an asset is added to the project, we will extend from the `AssetPostprocessor`, a class that will trigger several events when an asset is imported to the project depending on whether the asset is a 3D model, an audio, or a texture. In this example, our focus is to detect when a texture is imported, so we will add two methods. The first one is `OnPreprocessTexture`, which triggers before the importing process initiates. This is the perfect place to add the code related to configuring the settings of the imported asset. The second one is called the `OnPostprocessTexture` method. This method is similar to `OnPreprocessTexture`, except this one isn't called until the asset is imported. The final asset is passed as a parameter on this method, and this is a good place to do something with it such as generating a new prefab using this asset, reallocating the asset in a specific folder, and so on.

As you can see in the code, we are just printing logs using the `assetPath` variable. This contains the pathname of the asset being imported.

To test this, pick from the book contents an image, **Bg_OrangeSky.png** for example, and drop that into the root of the project. You will see a couple of logs in the console, as follows:

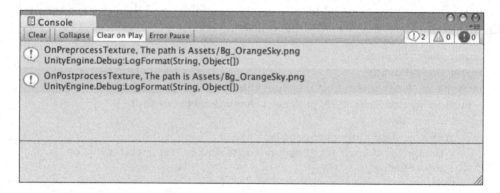

Our class works and captures the changes when a texture is added to the project. Using this as a base, we can make something more interesting to improve our import pipeline.

 To become familiar with all the available methods from the `AssetPostprocessor` class, visit `http://docs.unity3d.com/ScriptReference/AssetPostprocessor.html`.

Improving the import pipeline

It is possible to change the default settings Unity applies for all the assets added to the project and also, depending on your creativity and the pipeline you want to build, you can use different import settings for the asset based on filename, location, and so on.

Overwriting the background and level piece assets settings

Do you remember the asset we dropped into the project to test the script we created in the last section? Let's check its properties in the inspector:

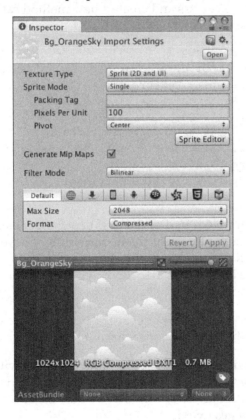

 When you create a new project and select the option **2D** or **3D**, it tells Unity how to deal with the assets imported, in this case, for example, the project uses **2D** so all the images are imported as Sprites instead of textures.

One thing that all projects should have is a file naming and folder structure convention; it makes things more organized and is really important if you have other people working with you. If a texture is dropped in Assets/Art/Bg, we are going to assume the texture is a background for the video game.

To satisfy our requirements, we will set up three things:

- **Texture Type:** This must be a Sprite, and should be independent if the project is configured as a 2D or 3D project.
- **Generate Mip Maps**: These are not necessary. Disabling them will reduce the file size of the texture or sprite.
- **Pivot**: This is required to have the pivot on the bottom-left corner.

Open the `TexturePipeline` class and create a new method called `PreprocessBg` with the following code:

```
private void PreprocessBg () {
    TextureImporter importer = assetImporter as TextureImporter;
    importer.textureType = TextureImporterType.Sprite;
    TextureImporterSettings texSettings = new
    TextureImporterSettings();
    importer.ReadTextureSettings(texSettings);
    texSettings.spriteAlignment = (int) SpriteAlignment.BottomLeft;
    texSettings.mipmapEnabled = false;
    importer.SetTextureSettings(texSettings);
}
```

The `assetImporter` variable is part of the `AssetPostprocessor` class and gives us access to the properties of the asset we are importing. As we are dealing with textures, we must cast the `assetImporter` variable to a `TextureImporter` (in other scenarios, you may like to use the `AudioImporter` or `ModelImporter` parameter for audio or 3D models respectively).

Using an instance of the `TextureImporterSettings` class, we can access the settings of this asset and make the modifications we want.

The most important thing to always keep in mind is to start with the method `ReadTextureSettings` and finish with the method `SetTextureSettings` in order to avoid unexpected results. Basically, with this we take the current configuration of the asset and make the changes over it.

Now, let's call this method inside the `OnPreprocessTexture` method by adding a rule based on the path of the asset:

```
private void OnPreprocessTexture () {
Debug.LogFormat("OnPreprocessTexture, The path is {0}",
assetPath);
    if (assetPath.StartsWith ("Assets/Art/Bg")) {
    PreprocessBg ();
  }
}
```

Remove the **Bg_OrangeSky.png** asset we originally added and add it again to the project, but this time, ensure that you drop the asset inside the `Assets/Art/Bg` folder and check the properties.

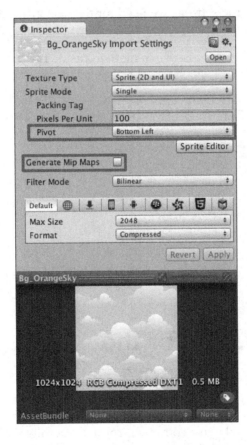

We changed the default settings based on our video game project requirements. Now, we will repeat the same procedure, but for the art used by the level piece prefabs:

```
private void PreprocessLevelPieces() {
    TextureImporter importer = assetImporter as TextureImporter;
    importer.textureType = TextureImporterType.Sprite;
    TextureImporterSettings texSettings = new TextureImporterSettings();
    importer.ReadTextureSettings(texSettings);
    texSettings.spriteAlignment = (int) SpriteAlignment.Center;
    texSettings.mipmapEnabled = false;
    importer.SetTextureSettings(texSettings);
}
```

This is pretty similar to the settings we used for the backgrounds. The only difference is that we keep the pivot of the image in the center.

Now, add the `PreprocessLevelPieces` method inside the `OnPreprocessTexture` method as follows:

```
private void OnPreprocessTexture () {
Debug.LogFormat("OnPreprocessTexture, The path is {0}",
assetPath);
if( assetPath.StartsWith( "Assets/Art/Bg" ) ) {
    PreprocessBg();
    } else if(
    assetPath.StartsWith( "Assets/Art/Platformer" ) ) {
    PreprocessLevelPieces();
    }
}
```

With this approach, we don't need to worry about the settings of the art assets anymore.

Using a DLL file for the AssetPostprocessors

If you have your video game in a production pipeline, you must consider placing all your AssetPostprocessors in a prebuilt DLL file in the project instead of in scripts. This is because when you have a compile error in one of the project scripts, it will lead to assets being imported differently.

The DLL approach helps us to ensure that they can always be executed even if the scripts of our project have compile errors.

In this section, you will learn how to create a DLL file in MonoDevelop using the scripts we created in the previous sections.

Creating and setting up a DLL project

DLLs are **Dynamic Link Libraries**; this means that they're linked to your program at runtime instead of compile time.

Usually we create new scripts from Unity, but in this case we will interact directly with MonoDevelop. Run the application, and create a new solution by navigating to **File | New | Solution** from the menu bar. This opens the following window:

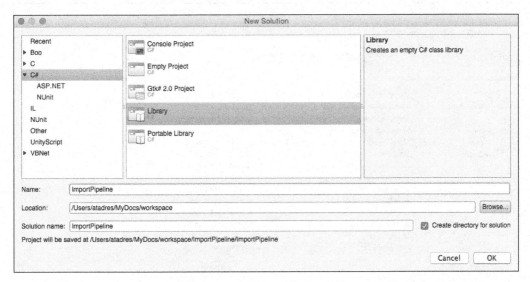

Here, select **C#** in the left column and then the **Library** option from the center column. Name this project `ImportPipeline` and then click on the **OK** button. A new script called `MyClass.cs` is created. For our purposes just remove that file.

To access the Unity API from the DLL, we must import the **UnityEngine** and **UnityEditor** assemblies into the project references. These assemblies, or DLLs, are inside the Unity application folder.

In MonoDevelop, go to the menu bar and navigate to **Project | Edit References**. This will open a new window with several tabs. Select **.Net Assembly** to access a file explorer interface.

Depending on the operating system you are using, the DLLs we are looking for will be located in `Applications/Unity/Unity.app/Content/Framework/Managed`, if you are using OSX or in `Program Files\Unity\Editor\Data\Managed` if you are using Windows.

Take into consideration that your project will use specific DLLs based on the version of Unity you have. This is important if you want to reuse your DLLs in other video game projects.

Let's take a look at the following screenshot:

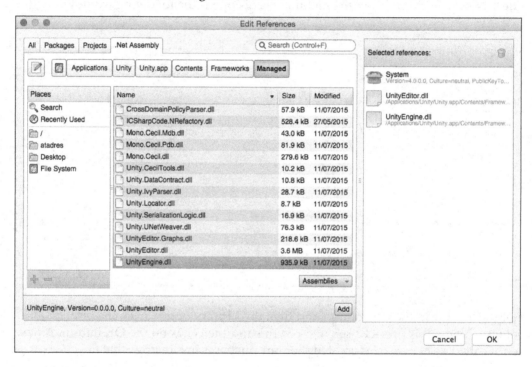

Click on the **UnityEditor.dll** and **UnityEngine.dll** assemblies to add the references, and then click on the **OK** button.

You are almost ready. The last thing to do is to verify the current Target Framework of this solution. Go to the menu bar and navigate to **Project | ImportPipeline options** (this changes depending on the name of the project):

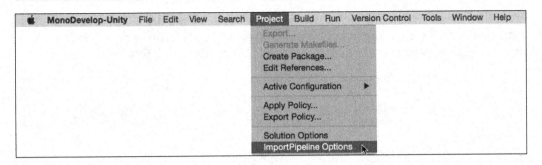

In the **Project Options** window, on the right-hand side, navigate to **Build | General** and then check whether **Target Framework** is set to **Mono / .NET 4.0**.

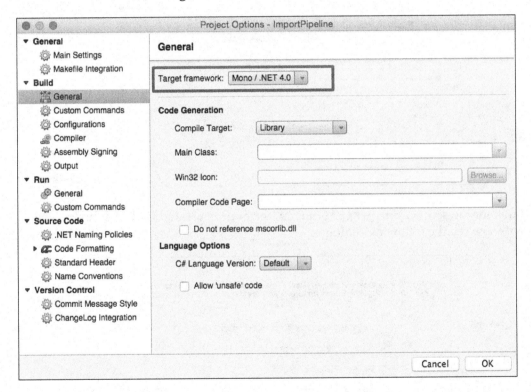

Finally, click on the **OK** button.

From the MonoDevelop menu bar, navigate to **View | Visual Design**. This will open a side bar with the solution structure in the main window. Now, a right-click on the **ImportPipeline** project and navigate to **Add | Add Files...**, as follows:

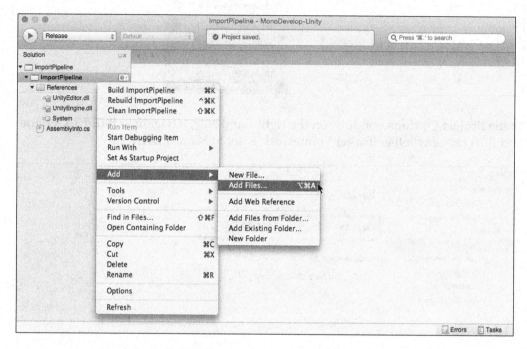

Look for the script `TexturePipeline.cs`, the one we created in Run & Jump. You will now see the following dialog:

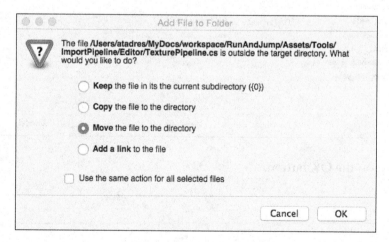

Select **Move the file to the directory** and then click on **OK**. The script will appear in your DLL project now:

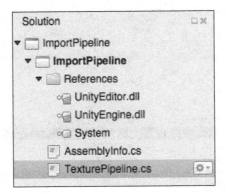

Integrating the DLL file to the main project

Now, to build the DLL file, check whether the **Release** option is selected in the top-left corner of MonoDevelop.

> By default, there are two types of configurations: **Debug** and **Release**. The first type includes debug information in the compiled files (allowing easy debugging) while the second type usually has optimizations enabled.

Then, go to the MonoDevelop menu bar and navigate to **Build | Build ImportPipeline** (this changes depending on the name of the project).

Once the solution is built, navigate to `ImportPipeline/bin/Release`, where the `ImportPipeline.dll` file was created:

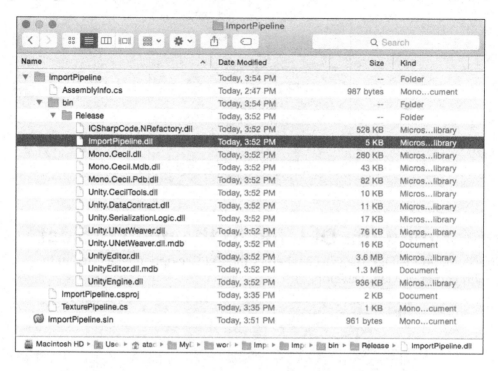

This DLL is the file that we need to add to our Unity video game project. Open the `Run & Jump` project and copy and paste the `ImportPipeline.dll` file inside the `Tools/ImportPipeline/Editor`.

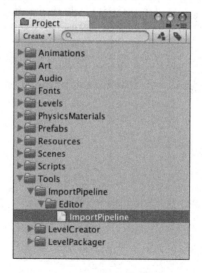

Adding the DLL file inside the `Editor` folder will make it available only for the editor context. You can check this by looking at the **Inspector** window when you select the DLL file, as shown in the following screenshot:

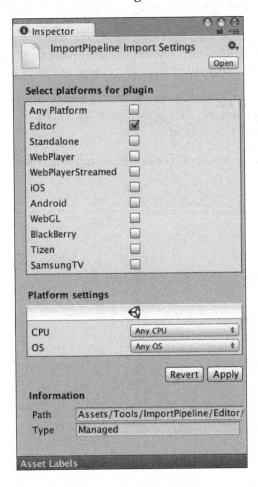

Now our import pipeline is ready!

Summary

In this chapter, you learned how to use the `AssetPostprocessor` in your projects, allowing you to control what is happening every time you drop an asset into your project.

The main idea behind using these classes is to deal with asset settings, which are very important to keep your project up and running without problems.

We did a very basic example in this chapter but the main idea remains, and it is up to you to make simple or complex things using the `AssetPostprocessor` to satisfy the requirements of your team and your project.

In the next chapter we are going to continue automating things now in the build pipeline.

Improving the Build Pipeline

9

Creating builds of your video game in Unity is easy, you just have to select the platform you want to target and then press a button. However, if you want to add some ad hoc features to your project necessities, you can customize this process.

We will experiment with upgrades to the build pipeline covering the basics, so you can use this as a starting point for your own projects later.

In this chapter, we will cover the following topics:

- Using Git
- The BuildPipeline class
- EditorPrefs
- Executing external scripts
- Using AppBlade

Overview

Nowadays, the life cycle of a video game project requires constants updates. In the past, as soon the video game was released, there was no scope for improvising or fixing bugs, but now developers have the opportunity to improve the game play or fix bugs by making new releases.

Before having a release candidate, it is important to create and share builds of the video game as it allows team members and testers to give you feedback on different topics that will affect the quality of the final result.

You may notice that the build creation process is something that repeats over and over, so it is natural to think of ways to automate this.

Defining the chapter goals

In this chapter, we will cover a few possible improvements for a build pipeline, enabling the reader to extrapolate and adapt all that they have learned to their own project.

The goals here are as follows:

- Allowing direct creation of builds
- Using external scripts to enhance the pipeline capabilities
- Integrating AppBlade for the distribution of mobile platform builds

Preparing the environment

We need to create a few folders to keep our development organized. Inside the Tools folder, create a new folder called AppBuilder, and then match the folder structure, as shown in the following screenshot:

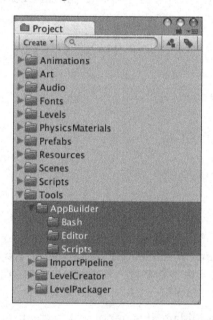

Automating the BuildPipeline class

The Build Pipeline varies depending on the project, but the core remains the same. You execute a few tasks before you create a build (or several ones), and then you do something with them.

We will start with the basics, generating a build using editor scripting and then creating several ones for different platforms with just one click.

Adjusting the player settings

Usually, before creating a build in Unity, you navigate to **File | Build Settings...** and click on **Player Settings** in the window that appears:

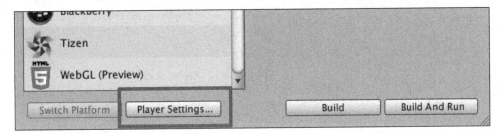

This will display all the properties that you can set for your build in the **Inspector** window, such as **Company name**, **Application name**, version, and so on:

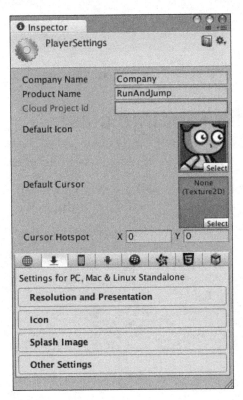

We can access and set all these parameters using the `PlayerSettings` class, which is part of the `UnityEditor` namespace.

Create a new script called `BuildSettings.cs` inside `Tools/AppBuilder/Editor` and copy the following code into the script:

```
using UnityEditor;

namespace AppBuilder {
  public class BuildSettings {

    public static void UpdateSettings () {
      // General
      PlayerSettings.companyName = "Packtpub";
      PlayerSettings.productName = "Run And Jump";
      PlayerSettings.bundleVersion = "1.0";

      // Android
      PlayerSettings.bundleIdentifier = "com.
      packtpub.runandjump";
    }
  }
}
```

Here, we just modified a few properties, but you get the idea.

Using the BuildPipeline class

The `BuildPipeline` class is part of the `UnityEditor` namespace and lets you programmatically make video games builds or Asset Bundles.

For the goal we want to achieve, we will use the method called `BuildPlayer`. Using this method is equivalent to pressing the button **Build** in the **Build Settings** window:

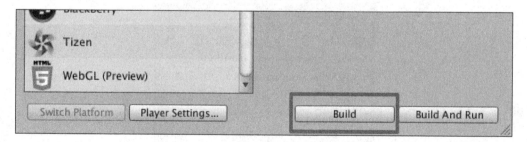

This method receives the following parameters:

- `levels`: This is an array of scenes to be included in the build
- `locationPathName`: This is the path where the application will be built
- `target`: This is the platform for the build we want to create
- `options`: These are additional build options, such as whether to run the built player

Regarding the `target` parameter, there are so many platforms you can deploy with Unity and their number grows every time with each new version available.

The following table shows the platforms supported in Unity 5.x:

Mobile	Desktop	Console	Web
iOS	Windows	PS3	Web Player
Android	Windows Store Apps	PS4	Web GL
Windows Phone 8	Mac	PSVita	
BlackBerry 10	Linux/Steam OS	Xbox 360	
Tizen		Xbox One	
		Wii U	

With all these alternatives, it is tempting to launch our game across multiple platforms to increase our number of users. Having access to the `BuildPlayer` method allows us to automate the creation of all these builds. Let's start coding!

Create a script called `Builder.cs` inside the folder `Tools/AppBuilder/Editor` and add the following code:

```
using UnityEngine;
using UnityEditor;
using System.Collections.Generic;

namespace AppBuilder {
  public class Builder {

    private static string[] GetEnabledScenes () {
      List<string> scenes = new List<string>();
      foreach (EditorBuildSettingsScene s in
      EditorBuildSettings.scenes) {
        if (s.enabled) {
          scenes.Add(s.path);
        }
```

```
        }
        return scenes.ToArray();
      }
    }
  }
```

The first thing to solve is what Unity scenes are going to be in the build. For this, we write the method GetEnabledScenes, which looks for all the enabled scenes that appear in the **Build Settings** window using the UnityEditor class EditorBuildSettings. This returns an array with strings, where each string is the path of a scene.

Then, in order to keep everything organized, we will create a folder to save all the builds we make.

Add the following code inside the Builder class:

```
private static string buildFolderPath = Application.dataPath +
"/../Build";

public static void CreateBuildFolder () {
  if (System.IO.Directory.Exists (buildFolderPath)) {
    System.IO.Directory.Delete (buildFolderPath, true);
  }
  System.IO.Directory.CreateDirectory (buildFolderPath);
}
```

Here, we defined a variable and a new method. The class Application, which is part of the UnityEngine namespace, contains static methods for looking up information about our application, that is, our video game project. The method dataPath contains the absolute path of the Assets folder of the Unity project. So, in this case, a folder with the name Build that is located at the same level as the Assets folder will be the container of the builds.

The method CreateBuildFolder does exactly this, creates a new folder based in the variable buildFolderPath. Every time we make a build, this folder will be deleted and created again.

If you want to use this code as a base for your own projects, you can make improvements such as deleting only the builds you want to rebuild instead of deleting all of them. However, for now, let's keep that behavior.

Time to use the `BuildPipeline` class. Add the following block of code inside the `Builder` class:

```
public static void Build(BuildTarget target, string buildName) {
    BuildSettings.UpdateSettings();
    string[] scenes = GetEnabledScenes();
    string buildFullPath;

    buildFullPath = buildFolderPath + "/" + target + "/" +
    buildName;
    BuildPipeline.BuildPlayer (scenes, buildFullPath, target,
    BuildOptions.None);
}
```

Here we have a method called `Build` that receives an array of the `BuildTarget`, an enum that defines which platform we need, and the name of the build. Inside this method, we make use of the `BuildPlayer` parameter.

The core is ready. So, we will now call this method from an editor window.

Creating an editor window and learning about EditorPrefs to persist data

Basically, here we are creating a tool that helps control the `BuildPipeline` class. For interacting with this tool, we will use an editor window. We will render a list of checkboxes, each representing a target platform.

Inside `Tools/AppBuilder/Editor`, create a new script called `SettingsWindow.cs`, and copy the following code:

```
using UnityEngine;
using UnityEditor;
using System.Collections.Generic;

namespace AppBuilder {
    public class SettingsWindow : EditorWindow {

        private Dictionary<BuildTarget, string> _targets;
        private const string Prefix = "AppBuilder_";

        public static SettingsWindow instance;

        public static void ShowSettings () {
            instance = (SettingsWindow)EditorWindow.GetWindow
            (typeof(SettingsWindow));
```

```
        instance.titleContent = new GUIContent ("AppBuilder");
    }

    private void OnEnable() {
      InitTargets();
    }

    private void InitTargets() {
      _targets = new Dictionary<BuildTarget, string>();
      _targets.Add(BuildTarget.StandaloneWindows, "Windows");
      _targets.Add(BuildTarget.StandaloneLinux, "Linux");
      _targets.Add(BuildTarget.StandaloneOSXIntel, "MacOS");
      _targets.Add(BuildTarget.Android, "Android");
    }
  }
}
```

We added a method called `ShowSettings` to display the editor window and also an `OnEnable` event. This last one calls a method that creates a dictionary with all the `BuildTarget` enums we want to use for the `AppBuilder` paired with a string with a "friendly" name for the platform.

To deal with the checkboxes, that is toggle, we will use the following two methods:

```
    private void DrawPlatformToggle(BuildTarget target, string label)
    {
    // We try to make a unique key for this EditorPref variable
      string key = Prefix + target.ToString();
    // We define false the default value of the EditorPref if this is
    not defined
      bool currentValue = EditorPrefs.GetBool(key, false);
      EditorPrefs.SetBool(key, GUILayout.Toggle(currentValue, label));
    }

    private bool GetPlatformToggleValue(BuildTarget target) {
      string key = Prefix + target.ToString();
      return EditorPrefs.GetBool(key, false);
    }
```

The `DrawPlatformToggle()` method wraps the method `Toggle` from the `GUILayout` class to render checkboxes, but there are a few more interesting things there.

When you create an editor window, you can make changes to the exposed variables using GUI components, such as a `FoatField` variable or, in this case, a `Toggle`. These changes will remain until you close the editor window. So, in order to make them persist, you have two options:

- **Scriptable Object**: This is created in case you want to make changes to a part of the project

- **EditorPrefs**: This is used in case you want to make changes to the environment of each developer

 On MacOS, the EditorPrefs values are stored in `~/Library/Preferences/com.unity3d.UnityEditor.plist`. On Windows, the EditorPrefs values are stored in the registry under the `HKCU\Software\Unity Technologies\UnityEditor` key.

An `EditorPref` value requires the creation of a key (just a unique string name to identify the variable we want to set or get) and then you can use that key to set or save the following types:

- Int
- Float
- Bool
- Strings

In our case, we use this with a Bool to represent the state of the toggle, using the methods `GetBool()` and `SetBool()` (you can expect the same kind of naming convention for the rest of the types).

Finally, the method `GetPlatformToggleValue()` will help us to get that value back and use it in the final part of this editor window — the button that generates all the builds we checked.

Let's add the rest of the code to the class `SettingsWindow`:

```
private void OnGUI () {
  DrawPlatformsGUI();
  DrawButtonsGUI();
}

private void DrawPlatformsGUI() {
  EditorGUILayout.LabelField("Platforms", EditorStyles.boldLabel);
  EditorGUILayout.BeginVertical("box");
```

```
      foreach(KeyValuePair<BuildTarget, string> entry in _targets) {
        DrawPlatformToggle(entry.Key, entry.Value);
      }
      EditorGUILayout.EndVertical();
  }

  private void DrawButtonsGUI() {
    if(GUILayout.Button("Build",GUILayout.Height(40))) {
      StartBuildProcess();
    }
  }

  private void StartBuildProcess() {
    Builder.CreateBuildFolder();
  // We iterate over the toggle values to check what to build
    foreach(KeyValuePair<BuildTarget, string> entry in _targets) {
      if(GetPlatformToggleValue(entry.Key)) {
        Builder.Build(entry.Key, "build");
      }
    }
    EditorUtility.DisplayDialog ("AppBuilder", "Build process has
    finished!", "Ok");
  }
```

This part must be familiar to you based on what we did in *Chapter 4, Creating Editor Windows*. Here, we added the GUI to the editor window and called the methods from the Builder class to make the builds.

The last thing to do is to make a menu item display in this window. Create a script called MenuItems.cs inside the folder Tools/AppBuilder/Editor and add the following code:

```
using UnityEditor;

namespace AppBuilder {
  public class MenuItems {

    [MenuItem ("Tools/AppBuilder/Show Settings")]
    private static void ShowSettings () {
      SettingsWindow.ShowSettings();
    }
  }
}
```

Save and wait for Unity to compile. Then, in the Unity menu, naviagte to **Tools | AppBuilder | Show Settings**:

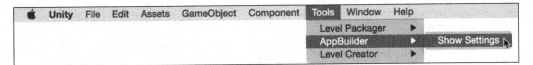

This will display the editor window we created:

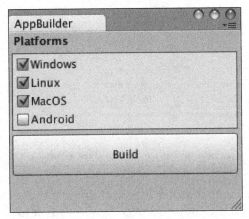

For now, select the platforms **Windows**, **Linux**, and **MacOS**. Then, click on the **Build** button. Unity will start the process of creating the builds for all the platform in sequence. When the process is done, you will see a dialog window like this:

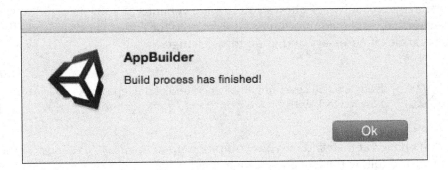

If you go to the `Build` folder located in the root of your project folder, you will see the following three builds there:

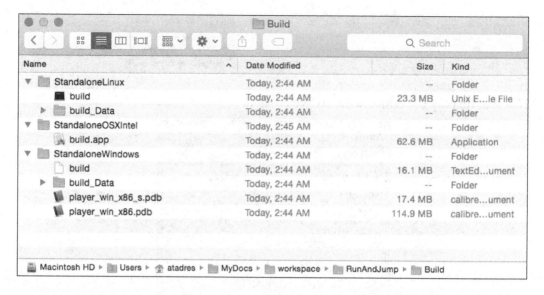

You have to admit, this is much faster than creating the builds using the **Build Settings** window and building it through code allows you to hook more actions in the process.

Adding version control to your project

The version control software allows you to have versions of your project that show the changes that were made by you or your team to the code over time, and allows you to backtrack if necessary and undo those changes.

> Here, we will cover only the generation of the repository. To learn how to work with Git, visit https://git-scm.com/.

If you don't have Git installed on your computer, go to https://git-scm.com/downloads and follow the installation instructions there.

If you aren't using Git in the project, open a terminal (in Windows, you can use Git Bash) and then go to the root of the project Run & Jump:

Now, execute the following to begin using Git in your project:

```
$ git init
```

Here you create a Git repository. Before we continue, create a file called `.gitignore` in the root of your project and add the following content to it:

```
[Ll]ibrary/
[Tt]emp/
[Oo]bj/
[Bb]uild/

# Autogenerated VS/MD solution and project files
*.csproj
*.unityproj
*.sln
*.suo
*.tmp
*.user
*.userprefs
*.pidb
*.booproj

# Unity3D generated meta files
*.pidb.meta

# Unity3D Generated File On Crash Reports
sysinfo.txt

# MacOS Files
*.DS_Store
```

This will help us to avoid version controlling unnecessary files. This `.gitignore` file is specifically for Unity video game projects.

Then, in the terminal, execute this:

```
$ git add -A
$ git commit -a -m 'First Commit'
```

Here you added all the files to version controlling and then generated a commit with the name "First Commit". The commit is a snapshot of your project, so each time you make changes, you can create a new commit.

Execute the following:

```
$ git log -1
```

You will get the following output:

```
1. bash
atadres at Jarvis in ~/MyDocs/workspace/RunAndJump on master*
$ git log -1
commit c55caac237c205c6694f6952aa608bf77e4df71b
Author: Angelo Tadres <me@angelotadres.com>
Date:   Thu Aug 20 22:54:42 2015 -0300

    First Commit
```

Each commit has a unique hash, so we will use this to identify our builds. This means that if somebody finds an error on the build, it's easy to go to the specific commit to check what's going on.

Interacting with external scripts

In this section, you will learn how to call bash scripts from Unity and how to integrate this to our pipeline.

 The examples here are using bash scripts (OS X). You can extend these to be used on Windows by your own

Displaying the build information in the video game

We will add a tiny text in the title screen containing two things:

- **Hash**: This corresponds to the commit used to create the build
- **Date**: This corresponds to the date on which the build is created

This information, which we will call the build info, will be updated every time you create a new build.

If you start the game in the Title scene, you will see a little text **Build Info** in the top-left corner

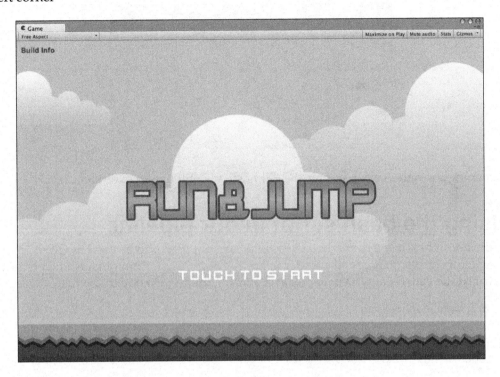

Let's replace this text. First, create a new script called `BuildInfo.Autogenerated.cs` inside `Tools/AppBuilder/Scripts` and add the following code:

```
namespace AppBuilder {
  public class BuildInfo {
    public const string Hash = "";
    public const string Date = "";
  }
}
```

Now, open the `TitleScene.cs` script and overwrite the method `SetBuildInfo` as follows:

```
private void SetBuildInfo() {
  string info = "";
  info += "Hash: " + AppBuilder.BuildInfo.Hash +"\n";
  info += "Date: " + AppBuilder.BuildInfo.Date;
  BuildInfoText.text = info;

}
```

If you run the video game, you will see the labels for the **Hash** and the **Date**.

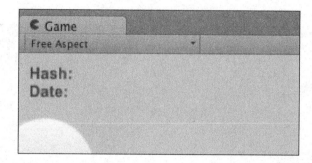

Obtaining the date is easy, but for the Git hash, we will use an external script.

Using the bash script in our pipeline

Unity doesn't allow us to create text files that are not meant to be used as C# or JavaScript scripts, so access the folder `Assets/Tools/Bash` from outside and create a new text file called `mac_githash.sh` and add the following code to the file:

```
#! /usr/bin/env sh

SHORT_HASH="$( git log --pretty=format:'%h' -n 1 )"
echo $SHORT_HASH
```

This script grabs the current commit hash and returns a short version of it. So, instead of 40 characters, this will return something like `4cd9c3a`.

> You must give execution permission to this script in order to make it work.

To use and call these kinds of scripts from Unity, we will create a utility method that receives the path from the script and parameters, if necessary.

Inside the `Builder` class, add the following method:

```
private static string ExecuteCommand (
  string command, string arguments = "") {
    System.Diagnostics.Process pProcess = new
    System.Diagnostics.Process ();
    pProcess.StartInfo.FileName = command;
    pProcess.StartInfo.Arguments = arguments;
    pProcess.StartInfo.UseShellExecute = false;
    pProcess.StartInfo.RedirectStandardOutput = true;
    pProcess.Start ();
    string strOutput = pProcess.StandardOutput.ReadToEnd ();
    pProcess.WaitForExit ();
    return strOutput;
  }
)
```

In this method we use the `Process` class, which is part of the .Net API. This provides access to local and remote processes and enables you to start and stop local system processes.

Basically, we are creating a `Process` instance here, setting its properties, and finally executing it. If there is any kind of output, that will be returned by the method as a string.

For each bash script we want to use, we must use this method to integrate it with our editor scripting code.

Still in the `Builder` class, we now create a new method to wrap the scripts we created in the folder `Bash`:

```
private static string batchPath = Application.dataPath +
"/Tools/AppBuilder/Bash";

private static string GitHash () {
  string command = batchPath + "/mac-githash.sh";
  string output = ExecuteCommand (command);
  // We trim the output to remove new lines at the end.
  return output.Trim();
}
```

Now, getting the Git hash is transparent for the rest of the tool because all the interactions with script are encapsulated.

Remember the `BuildInfo.Autogenerated.cs` script we created at the beginning? The main idea for that class is to be overwritten in the pipeline process with the following method:

```
private static void GenerateBuildInfo () {
  string content = "";
  string hash = GitHash();
  string date = System.DateTime.Now.ToString();;
  content += "namespace AppBuilder {\n";
  content += "\tpublic class BuildInfo {\n";
  content += string.Format("\t\tpublic const string Hash =
  \"{0}\";\n", hash);
  content += string.Format("\t\tpublic const string Date =
  \"{0}\";\n", date);
  content += "\t}";
  content += "}";

  string buildInfoPath = Application.dataPath +
  "/Tools/AppBuilder/Scripts/BuildInfo.Autogenerated.cs";
  System.IO.File.WriteAllText (buildInfoPath, content);
}
```

As we have two assemblies, one for the Editor and another for the video game, we can make modifications of this kind in the code of the video game using an Editor script without problem. The class modification will happen before compiling the video game.

Update the `Build` method:

```
public static void Build(BuildTarget target, string buildName) {
  BuildSettings.UpdateSettings();
  GenerateBuildInfo ();
  string[] scenes = GetEnabledScenes();
  string buildFullPath;

  buildFullPath = buildFolderPath + "/" + target + "/" +
  buildName;
  BuildPipeline.BuildPlayer (scenes, buildFullPath, target,
  BuildOptions.None);
}
```

Now, repeat the process to generate a new build and run it. You will see the build info on the video game title scene:

In the next section, we will continue using a part of the tools we created here. However, we will now focus on adding distribution to the build pipeline.

Distributing your video game using AppBlade

In this section, you will learn how to integrate with **AppBlade** to our pipeline to distribute Android builds.

AppBlade is a platform for mobile application distribution, simplifying how you share your mobile applications or video games with your team and testers. Using the application available on Google Play and the AppStore, you can install and run your builds directly in your phone.

Creating an AppBlade account

The first thing to do is to create a new account on the AppBlade website. Open your favorite browser and go to `http://appblade.com`. There are several pricing alternatives, but the one we will use is Indie, which allows us to have 25 devices registered for free before we start paying $1 per additional device:

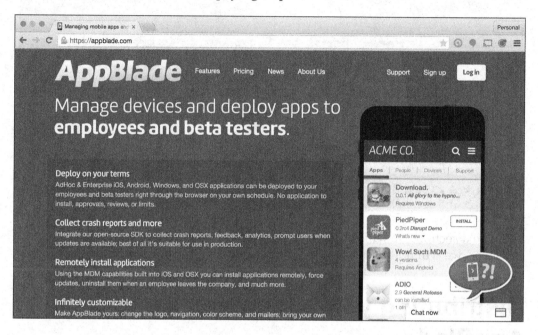

Click on the **Sign up** link and follow the steps to create an account. Appblade will ask you to confirm your e-mail before you continue, as soon as you are ready, you will see the main page. Click on the **New Project** button:

Here you need to complete information related to your new project, this includes the name and description. In this case, we use the name `Run And Jump`.

When you have finished, click on the **Create Project** button. Your project will appear in the main page of the project you created:

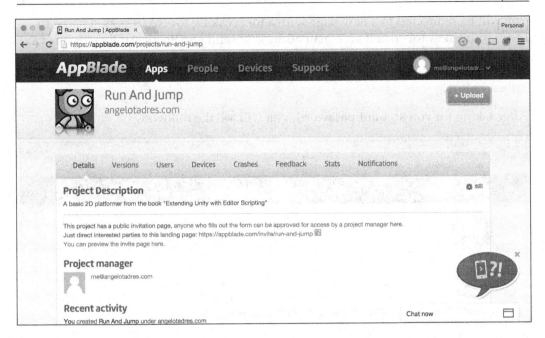

Uploading the build

Using the API of AppBlade, we will upload our builds directly to this platform. But before we do that, we need to generate a **CI Token**. This is a key that allows us to integrate AppBlade with other services.

In the main page of your project, go to the bottom and click on the link **Generate your first CI token**:

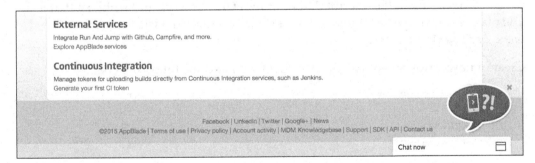

You will be redirected to a new page with a form asking for two things: a name to identify this new token and an e-mail address to send you an alert if there is an error uploading a build using this token. For this example, we used the name Run-and-Jump-builds. When you are ready, click on the **Create Continuous Integration Token** button.

After asking for you account password, you will see the following:

With this token, we are ready to perform the integration in Unity, so now is the time to code. We will use a Bash script that requires **cURL** to work and a library that lets you make HTTP requests. If you don't have cURL installed, visit http://curl.haxx.se/download.html.

Create a new script called mac-appblade.sh and add the following code:

```
#! /usr/bin/env sh

CI_TOKEN="$1"
BUNDLE_PATH="$2"
```

```
# Uploading to AppBlade...
curl -#
-H "Authorization: Bearer $CI_TOKEN"
-F "version[bundle]=@$BUNDLE_PATH" \
https://appblade.com/api/3/versions
```

This script receives the CI Token and the path to the build in order to upload. Using cURL we call the API of AppBlade to take care of the rest, pretty simple.

In the script `Builder.cs` we will create the wrapper for this, similar to the Git Hash:

```
private static string appBladeKey =
"7d90cf1850ff68bf127baca0780f3381";

private static string PublishOnAppblade (string build) {
   string command = batchPath + "/mac-appblade.sh";
   string arguments = string.Format("{0} {1}", appBladeKey, build);
   string output = ExecuteCommand (command, arguments);
   return output.Trim();
}
```

Inside the `PublishOnAppblade()` method, we execute the script passing two parameters, the CI Token and the path to the build.

Let's include this in the `Build` method:

```
public static void Build(BuildTarget target, string buildName) {
   BuildSettings.UpdateSettings();
   GenerateBuildInfo ();
   string[] scenes = GetEnabledScenes();
   string buildFullPath;

   buildFullPath = buildFolderPath + "/" + target + "/" +
   buildName;
   BuildPipeline.BuildPlayer (scenes, buildFullPath, target,
   BuildOptions.None);

   // Distribution
   if(target == BuildTarget.Android) {
     PublishOnAppblade (buildFullPath);
   }
}
```

Now, when trying to create a new Android Build, if you go to the AppBlade website at the end of the process you will see your build available to be downloaded. Take into consideration that the process will take longer depending on the size of the build and your internet connection:

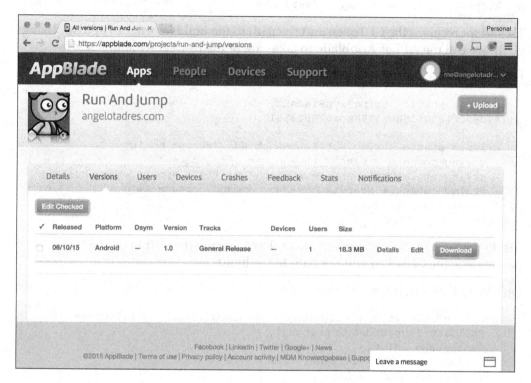

Summary

In this chapter, we worked on customizing the build pipeline for Run & Jump. We are now able to create builds for specific platforms, trigger several builds in sequence, and add information to the builds to make it easier to match with a commit in Git.

The example covered here was small but it is possible to extrapolate in order to have something better that matches with the reality of your own project.

Using external scripts in Unity allows you to have the flexibility to interact with other tools, at least the ones that allow you to use command lines to do stuff.

In the next chapter, we will talk about how to distribute your custom tools.

10

Distributing Your Tools

In the earlier chapters, we reviewed the basics of editor scripting and now you know the basics to create your own tools in Unity.

As soon you develop a tool, you will realize that this can be reused in one of your other projects or used by somebody else. For this reason, we will explore three different approaches to distributing your tools, including the process of publishing content in the Unity Asset store.

In this chapter, we will cover the following topics:

- Unity packages
- Git submodules
- Publishing and selling content in the Asset store

Overview

How you share or distribute tools across projects or teams is an important part of your development workflow. If you have invested time and resources solving a particular problem in a project using a custom tool, it makes sense to use it again in other projects too.

The challenge appears when you try to find the best way to do this distribution and also keep the tool updated. On the other hand, you need to know what happens if you decide to focus on the development of tools instead of video games and you want to distribute your tools, making money in the process.

In this chapter, you will learn how to use packages and Git submodules for custom tools distribution that are more suitable for sharing inside a team, and how to sell content in the Asset Store.

Defining the chapter goals

In this chapter, we will focus on tool distribution using the AppBuilder tool we created in the previous chapter as an example.

The goals here are:

- Creating and using a Unity Package
- Creating and using a Git submodule
- Using the Admin panel of the Asset Store to create a publisher's account and defining the information of the package to be submitted
- Using the Asset Store Tools to prepare the package
- Submitting the package to the Asset Store

Preparing the environment

In a normal development situation, if the custom tools that we will create are meant to be something reusable, the best decision is to deal with them as independent projects. Let's do this with the AppBuilder tool.

First, create a new Unity project with the name `AppBuilder` and then move the files related to this tool from the *Run & Jump* project here.

Your project must look like this:

We used this folder structure here just to match it to the structure we have in *Run & Jump*. However, as a good practice, always use a root folder with the name of the tool you want to share, if possible.

Here, we are assuming that you have the *Run & Jump* project integrated with Git. It is necessary that you go through the *Sharing code using Git submodules* section. After reallocating the AppBuilder files from the *Run & Jump* project, commit the change in *Run & Jump*.

Sharing code using a Unity Package

A Unity Package allows us to export and import collections of source code and project assets in a simple way.

For instance, if we have a Unity tool with several scripts, textures, and materials, it could be converted to a package. Then, when others use this tool in their project, importing the package replicates the original structure of assets and source files and helps to track file additions and duplications.

In this section, you will learn how to create and use a Unity Package.

Creating a package

The package creation process is very simple. In the AppBuilder project, select the root folder, the one with the name **Tools**, and then navigate to **Assets | Export Package...** in the Unity menu:

This will open a new window called **Exporting package**, where you can select which scripts or assets will go inside the package. In this case, everything must be selected.

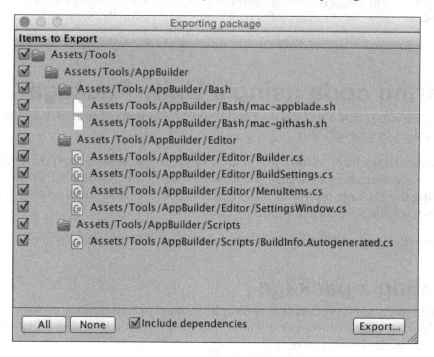

When you are ready, press the **Export...** button. This opens a save file dialog, where you need to choose the location and the name of the package:

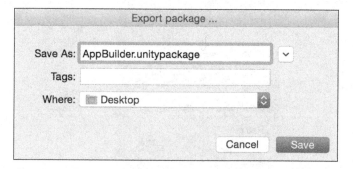

Name this AppBuilder.unitypackage and save it wherever you want. Hopefully, this will create a neat package containing all the necessary items to use the AppBuilder tool in any project.

Importing a package

To test the package we created, open the *Run & Jump* project. Here, you have two options to import the package:

1. Double-click on the package using the file explorer of your operating system.

2. In Unity, navigate to **Assets | Import Package | Custom Package...** in the Unity editor menu:

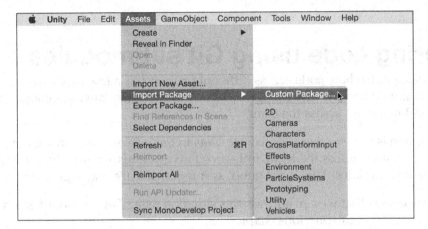

Under the **Custom Package...** option, you will find a list of Unity packages distributed with Unity.

3. After this, a new window will appear displaying all the content of the package:

4. Select all the files and folders from this package and then click on the **Import** button. This will copy all the content in your project.

 If you reimport the package, only the new and modified files (or folder) will appear in the list.

Now, you are ready to start using the AppBuilder in this project, or any project you want.

Sharing code using Git submodules

Using packages to share code across different projects has a few problems. These are hard to maintain because any change means a new package must be generated and distributed manually across the team.

Collaboration is not easy because fixes to bugs in the implementation are not necessarily shared across the team, unless you invest time to manually share the packages with updates. This is not good, as it requires extra management.

The good news is that we can address this situation using Git submodules as we started using Git in the previous chapter.

With submodules, you can maintain a Git repository as a subdirectory of another Git repository. This lets you clone another repository with a specific tool into your project and keep your commits separate.

In this section, we will make the AppBuilder tool a submodule used by *Run & Jump*.

Creating a submodule

We need to create a Git repository inside the AppBuilder project that only contains the files and folders we want to add in the submodule. This means that all the extra files and folders Unity creates won't be included here, for example, the project settings.

In this case, we need to open a terminal (in Windows, use Git bash or something similar) and remain in the root of the AppBuilder project:

Now execute the following commands:

```
$ cd Assets/Tools/AppBuilder
$ git init
```

Finally, make the first commit:

```
$ git add .
$ git commit -m 'First commit'
```

The last thing to do is to make this repository available using a repository hosting service such as GitHub.

 GitHub offers both paid plans for private repositories and free accounts. To learn how to publish your repository, visit `https://help.github.com/articles/adding-an-existing-project-to-github-using-the-command-line/`.

For this example, we hosted the AppBuilder tool in `https://github.com/angelotadres/AppBuilder`.

Now, we are ready to start using our submodule in the Run & Jump project.

Using a submodule

Right now, this is the current status of the Run & Jump project:

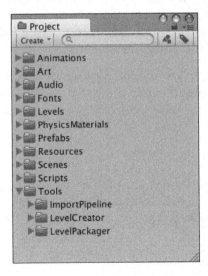

The AppBuilder folder will no longer be a part of the project because we will add this using a Git submodule.

In the terminal, go to the folder in which you have the Run & Jump project (this assumes that you already have this project under version control using Git).

Now, execute the following (replacing the last part with your submodule repository if you have it):

```
$ cd Assets/Tools
$ git submodule add git@github.com:angelotadres/AppBuilder.git
```

By default, the command submodule will add the subproject to a directory named the same as the repository, in this case, AppBuilder.

Finally, go back again to the root of the *Run & Jump* project and commit the changes.

Basically, the changes we made are the addition of a new folder and a new file called .gitmodules located in the root of the project. This file contains all the information about the submodules in your project.

Now, every time you have a change in your game, you can commit these changes normally. If you need to make a fix or change in the submodule, you need to go to that folder and deal with it as a normal repository. The good thing is that all the users of these tools are able to make improvements to them now.

After this, if you cloned or forked the main project or if you want to get the latest version of all the submodules, the only thing you need to do is execute these two commands in the root of your main project:

```
$ git submodule init
$ git submodule update
```

The first line initializes your local configuration file, that is, the .gitmodules file, and the second one fetches all the data from the project and checks out the appropriate commits listed in our main project.

To understand in depth how a submodule works, visit `https://git-scm.com/book/en/v2/Git-Tools-Submodules`.

Publishing in the Asset Store

Something that makes it easy to create new video games in Unity is the huge community it has and, of course, the Asset Store—a virtual store where you can find and buy prebuilt assets that can be imported directly into your video game project. If you are making a video game, you can look in the Asset Store and save time buying tools that help you with your development or assets that complement your gameplay requirements.

Additionally, this creates a new business line where instead of developing your own videogames, you can create tools of contents to help people to make video games and earn money from the sales in the process.

In this section, you will learn how to publish our stuff in the Asset Store, as an example, we will continue using the AppBuilder tool.

Installing the Asset Store Tools

To start, open the AppBuilder project, and then in the Unity menu navigate to **Window | Asset Store**. This will open the Asset Store window. In the top-right corner of this window, you have two options: **Login** and **Create Account**. If you have a Unity account proceed to log in, if not, just create a new one (don't worry, it's free!).

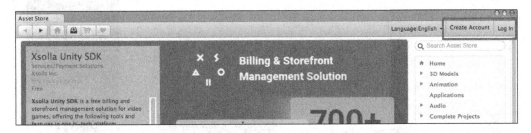

After this, scroll to the bottom of the main Asset Store page and click on the **Publish your stuff!** link (as an alternative, you can also search using the keyword `Asset Store Tools`):

Asset Store Tools is a package that adds the necessary scripts and editor tools to allow you to connect to the store's online publishing system. Click on the **Download** button and then import the package into your project, as shown in the following screenshot:

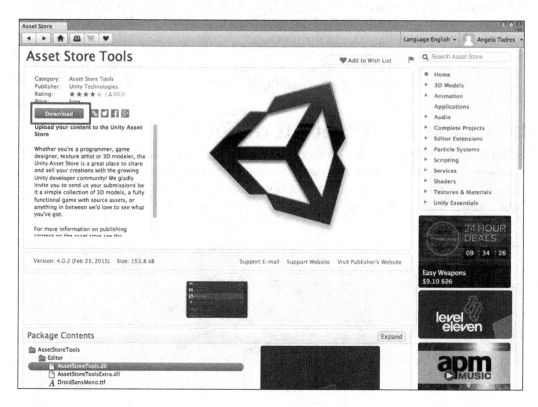

At the end of this process, if everything goes well, your project should have an extra folder called **AssetStoreTools**, which will look like this:

Also, the **Asset Store Tools** menu should appear in the Unity menu:

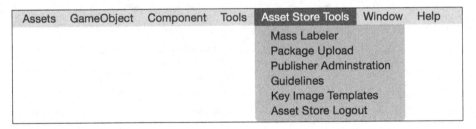

Save the project, and now you are ready to move on to the next step.

Becoming a publisher

It's time to be a publisher in the Asset Store platform, so go to the Unity menu and navigate to **Asset Store Tools | Publisher Administration**. This will open our default browser and send us to the **Unity Asset Store Publisher Administration**.

After logging in using your Unity account, you will be asked to create a Publisher account; proceed with it and you will see something like this:

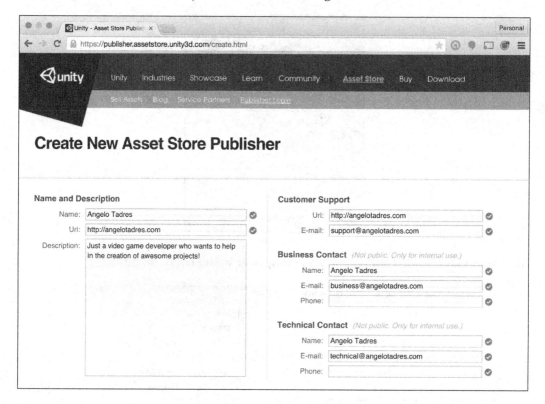

On this page, you will need to fill out the details related to your Publisher account such as your name, your website address, a brief description of yourself or your company, and contact information.

Additionally, you must provide two Key Images to complete your Publisher profile. The first one is a small image with 200 x 258 pixels, and the second one is a large image with 860 x 389 pixels. These images can be your company logo or something that makes it easier for your buyers to recognize you as a publisher.

Save the changes and now you are a publisher - well at least you have the account; however, to be a real publisher, you must publish content, so let's focus on that.

Uploading the package

In this section, we will prepare and upload the package we want to distribute in the Asset Store.

In the Publisher Admin, select the **Packages** tab, as shown here:

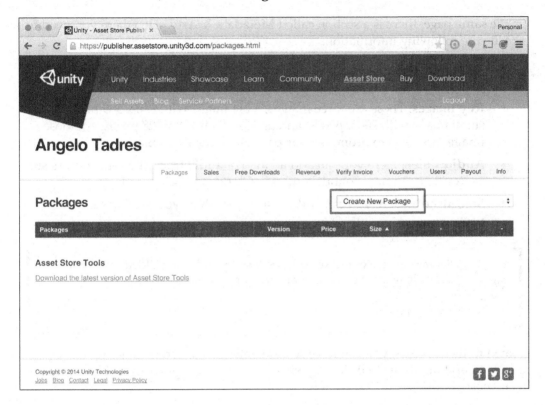

On this page, you will see a list of all your packages and their statuses. Click on the **Create New Package** button. This will send you to a new page where you will need to provide the following information about your package:

- **Version**: This is the version of your package, such as "1.0"
- **Version Changes**: This has all the changes to the current version
- **Category**: You must select one of the several categories the store has to categorize your package, such as Scripting/Network, Editor extensions, and so on.
- **Price USD**: You will have to specify the price in dollars or mark this as free.

> Remember, the Unity Asset Store takes 30 percent of the revenue from the sales. So, take this into consideration when you define the price. Also, it is recommended that you check the Asset Store for similar solutions to have an idea about what is the best price for your package.

On the same page, there is a section called **Metadata & Artwork**, where you need to provide the following information:

- **Metadata**: This includes the name of your package and a brief description of it.

- **Key Images**: These are three images; a big image with 860 x 389 pixels, a small image with 200 x pixels, and an icon with 128 x 128 pixels. All these images are used to promote your package in the Asset Store.

- **Audio/Video**: Here you can add a video or audio from different sources such as YouTube, Vimeo, SoundCloud, MixCloud, and Scketchfab.

- **Screenshots**: Here you can add all the screenshots you need to sell your package.

> For the creation of the Key Images, visit the following URL and download a Zip file with placeholder templates for Photoshop and Gimp:
>
> `http://unity3d.com/files/asset-store/asset-store-key-image-templates.zip`

Related to these values, you can have several entries in different languages. By default, everything must to be in English, but additionally you can add information in Japanese, Korean, and Chinese too.

As soon you complete filling all the information required here, go back to the **Packages** section. Now, you will see our **Package** listed:

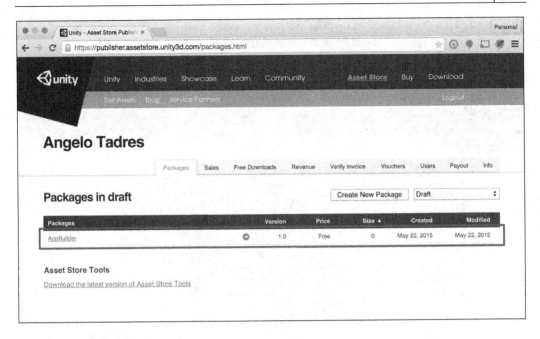

Our package is currently in draft status, or at least the data related to our package is. We are ready to submit our package to the platform!

Now that we have the entire package form filled out, we need to preview it to ensure that all the information is correct and the images look awesome. Click on the **Preview** button at the bottom of the form - the one that has a little arrow inside a circle, as shown here:

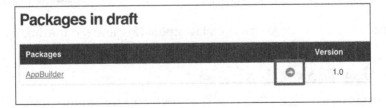

The Asset Store panel should appear with a test page showing your package information (the images used here are the placeholder templates).

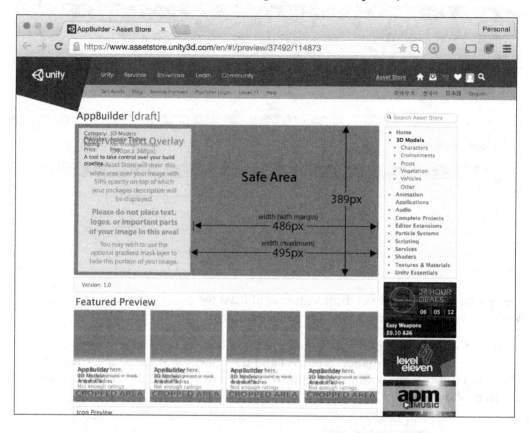

Now, it is time to go back to Unity and start uploading and submitting the package.

Using the Mass Labeler

In order to make it easier for other people to find your tool in the Asset Store, we will use the **Mass Labeler**, a way to add labels used as keywords in the Asset Store.

Back in the project, navigate to **Asset Store Tools | Mass Labeler**:

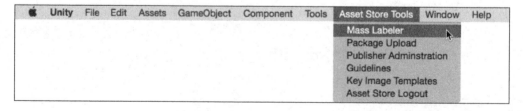

This will open the **Mass Labeler** editor window, where you must add all the labels (key words) that describe your tool. In this case, using the **New Label** field, we added the labels **Build** and **Automation**, as shown here:

Once you have added all the labels you need, click on each of them in the **Mass Labeler** editor window so they show as selected:

After this, select the main folder of your tool in the project browser, in this case, it is the folder AppBuilder, and click on the button **Apply to Selection**. That's it!

If you check the inspector of that folder, you will see the labels attached:

Uploading and submitting the project

Navigate to **Asset Store Tools | Package Upload**. This will open a new window where a list of all the package entries created in the Publisher Administration appears.

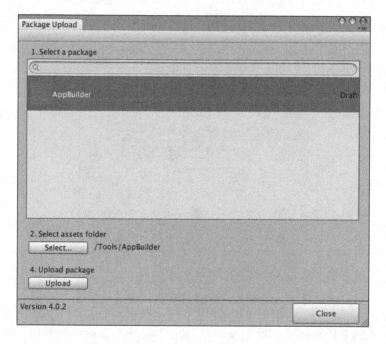

In this case, the only project listed is **AppBuilder**. So, the first step it to select that project and then select the root folder that has the contents of the package. Then, click on the **Upload** button.

You need to wait a moment while the package is uploaded. As soon the process finishes correctly, the following popup will appear:

Click on the **Ok** button and go to the publisher administration web page. In the **Packages** tab, select your package and then go to the bottom of the web page: you will see a checkbox with the label **I own the rights to sell these assets**:

Select the checkbox and then click on the **Submit packages for approval** button. If everything is OK, your package will change its state from **Draft** to **Pending Review**:

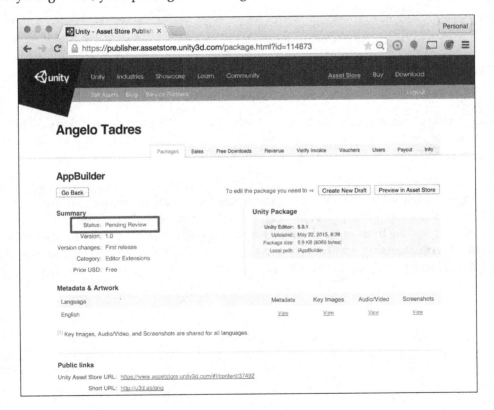

Now, all you have to do is grab a snack and sit back and wait for the review to be completed by the Unity staff.

Normally, this process will take around 5 business days, but in some cases it can take a bit longer. If you are submitting a package that provides a service, like an Ads service, you should expect it to take around two weeks to be reviewed as there are many things to consider such as the legal aspects involved.

If at this point you happen to discover that you have spelling mistakes or the screenshots of Key Images are wrong, don't worry, these things can all be modified in-place as long as you don't change the version number. You can then resubmit, but your package will go to the back of the queue for revision.

Take in consideration that if the mistake is related to the package, like a bug or something that needs to be tweaked, you must release a package under a new version number.

 In order to increase the probabilities of having your package accepted, take some time to read the submission guidelines available at `http://unity3d.com/asset-store/sell-assets/submission-guidelines`.

Summary

In this chapter, we concluded learning about how to share our tools.

Unity Packages are a good way to share tools. It is a feature supported natively by Unity and is flexible in terms of choosing which scripts or assets we want to use for that package.

However, if you are within a context where shared tools are a critical part of your development workflow, like a video game studio that tries to create standards and avoid reinventing the wheel on each project, using Git submodules is a better option, keeping the tools on each project updated and allowing collaboration for bug solving. If you are using another version control solution, there is a high probability that it will have something similar to this feature.

The last option reviewed was sharing using the Unity Asset Store. This creates new possibilities for anybody who has an idea for improving video game development in Unity, allowing developers to help other developers and earn money in the process.

This concludes this book. At this point, you have all the basics to start thinking of ways to improve your development workflow by creating custom tools. We have covered a lot of things but if you start investigating the Unity editor API, you will find more useful features that you can include in your tools. Most of them aren't well documented but you can always find support in the Unity community.

To finish, only one thing: don't be afraid to put Unity to use for your video games!

Index

Thank you for buying
Extending Unity with Editor Scripting

About Packt Publishing

Packt, pronounced 'packed', published its first book, *Mastering phpMyAdmin for Effective MySQL Management*, in April 2004, and subsequently continued to specialize in publishing highly focused books on specific technologies and solutions.

Our books and publications share the experiences of your fellow IT professionals in adapting and customizing today's systems, applications, and frameworks. Our solution-based books give you the knowledge and power to customize the software and technologies you're using to get the job done. Packt books are more specific and less general than the IT books you have seen in the past. Our unique business model allows us to bring you more focused information, giving you more of what you need to know, and less of what you don't.

Packt is a modern yet unique publishing company that focuses on producing quality, cutting-edge books for communities of developers, administrators, and newbies alike. For more information, please visit our website at www.packtpub.com.

Writing for Packt

We welcome all inquiries from people who are interested in authoring. Book proposals should be sent to author@packtpub.com. If your book idea is still at an early stage and you would like to discuss it first before writing a formal book proposal, then please contact us; one of our commissioning editors will get in touch with you.

We're not just looking for published authors; if you have strong technical skills but no writing experience, our experienced editors can help you develop a writing career, or simply get some additional reward for your expertise.

Unity 3D UI Essentials

ISBN: 978-1-78355-361-7   Paperback: 280 pages

Leverage the power of the new and improved UI system for Unity to enhance your games and apps

1. Discover how to build efficient UI layouts coping with multiple resolutions and screen sizes.

2. In-depth overview of all the new UI features that give you creative freedom to drive your game development to new heights.

3. Walk through many different examples of UI layout from simple 2D overlays to in-game 3D implementations.

Mastering Unity 4 Scripting [Video]

ISBN: 978-1-84969-614-2   Duration: 01:39 hours

Master Unity 4 gameplay scripting with this dynamic video course

1. Master Unity scripting using C# through step-by-step demonstrations.

2. Create enemy AI systems.

3. Script character animations.

4. Program directional and conditional sound effects as well as background music.

Please check **www.PacktPub.com** for information on our titles

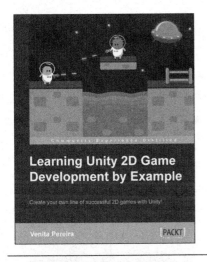

Learning Unity 2D Game Development by Example

ISBN: 978-1-78355-904-6   Paperback: 266 pages

Create your own line of successful 2D games with Unity!

1. Dive into 2D game development with no previous experience.

2. Learn how to use the new Unity 2D toolset.

3. Create and deploy your very own 2D game with confidence.

Unity 4.x Cookbook

ISBN: 978-1-84969-042-3   Paperback: 386 pages

Over 100 recipes to spice up your Unity skills

1. A wide range of topics are covered, ranging in complexity, offering something for every Unity 4 game developer.

2. Every recipe provides step-by-step instructions, followed by an explanation of how it all works, and alternative approaches or refinements.

3. Book developed with the latest version of Unity (4.x).

Please check **www.PacktPub.com** for information on our titles

CPSIA information can be obtained
at www.ICGtesting.com
Printed in the USA
FSOW04n1513090316
17830FS

9 781785 281853